The Chronicles of Major Peabody

Major Peabody

The Questionable Adventures
of a Wily Spendthrift,
a Politically Incorrect Curmudgeon,
an Unprincipled Wagerer and
an Obsessive Bird Hunter

by

Galen Winter

CCB Publishing
British Columbia, Canada

The Chronicles of Major Peabody: The Questionable Adventures of a Wily Spendthrift, a Politically Incorrect Curmudgeon, an Unprincipled Wagerer and an Obsessive Bird Hunter

Copyright ©2009 by Galen Winter
ISBN-13   978-1-926585-18-5
First Edition

Library and Archives Canada Cataloguing in Publication

Winter, Galen, 1926-
The chronicles of Major Peabody: the questionable adventures of a wily spendthrift, a politically incorrect curmudgeon, an unprincipled wagerer and an obsessive bird hunter / written by Galen Winter – 1st ed.
Short stories having first appeared in Shooting sportsman magazine.
ISBN 978-1-926585-18-5
1. Hunting stories, American. I. Title.
PS3573.I53675 C47 2009   813'.54   C2009-901226-X

The stories contained herein were first published in *Shooting Sportsman* magazine.

Extreme care has been taken to ensure that all information presented in this book is accurate and up to date at the time of publishing. Neither the author nor the publisher can be held responsible for any errors or omissions. Additionally, neither is any liability assumed for damages resulting from the use of the information contained herein.

All rights reserved. No part of this publication may be reproduced, stored in a retrieval system or transmitted in any form or by any means, electronic, mechanical, photocopying, recording or otherwise without the express written permission of the publisher. Printed in the United States of America and the United Kingdom.

Publisher: CCB Publishing
               British Columbia, Canada
               www.ccbpublishing.com

Dedication

For their assistance in funding his future hunting and fishing expeditions, the author gratefully acknowledges and sincerely thanks everyone who buys this book.

Contents

In the Beginning

I had been with the Smythe, Hauser, Engels & Tauchen law firm for nearly two years. During my Law School studies, I took every Contracts and contract related course offered by the university. I enjoyed that field of law and my grades showed it. The Smythe firm hired me and I specialized in Trusts and Estate Planning. I drafted Trusts Agreements and used my imagination in meeting the objectives and instructions of my clients. Frankly, I recall being pleased with my work.

When one is a young attorney in a large and prestigious Philadelphia Law Office, it can be dangerous to use one's imagination. The rules for advancement in such law firms are: sit down, keep your mouth shut, be pleasant to the men above you in the chain of command and don't become a threat to them by using your imagination. I was, therefore, somewhat concerned when called into the office of Mr. Robertson Smythe, the firm's senior partner.

Mr. Smythe asked me if I had plans for luncheon. I managed to say "Well, ah" before he told me to cancel them. I was sure I was about to be fired, told to clean out my desk and be gone within the hour. Instead Mr. Smythe handed me about ten inches of files, told me to study them and be back in his office at 11:45 for lunch. That visit to Mr. Smythe's office was the watershed moment of my career. The files he gave me represented the work Mr. Smythe did for William Henry Peabody.

The Peabody family had been in the New World since

Jamestown was founded. They looked upon the Mayflower people as Johnny-Come-Latelys. During the following four hundred years, the Peabody fortunes grew - at first from tobacco, then cotton and, for the past one hundred and fifty years, through banking and international commercial endeavors. The family reputation and its services as diplomats and philanthropists had a paralleled growth.

At our luncheon, Mr. Smythe told me he reviewed every trust document I had drafted during my first two years in the firm. He "found them interesting". Then he told me about Major Nathaniel Peabody, the only son of William Henry Peabody.

Nathaniel Peabody was born in Bogotá, Colombia, the son of the U S Embassy's First Secretary and the daughter of a Peruvian landowner who enjoyed a name and a reputation equal to that of the Peabody family. Every family has its black sheep. Nathaniel Peabody assumed that responsibility and was spectacularly successful in performing the duties of the office.

His special abilities in the Black Sheep Department were early recognized and he was sent to a succession of military academies in the United States in an effort to correct the lad's profligate and rebellious nature – "straighten him out" was the phrase the elder Peabody used.

Nathaniel looked upon the military academies' attempts to "straighten him out" as challenges and he behaved accordingly. After a single year of experience with him, each school admitted defeat and asked the elder Peabody to transfer him to another institution. One school Commandant recommended Nathaniel be transferred to a particular institution that required arrest, trial and a finding of "Guilty" as qualifications for admission.

During his school vacations and whenever he elected to

shun attendance at the military academies, Nathaniel visited his uncle, Calhoun Peabody. Uncle Calhoun lived in Georgia and had already disgraced the family by entering a trade. He had become a realtor during the Depression of the 1930's.

Due to widespread foreclosures, many Georgia farms had been abandoned and were owned by banks and insurance companies. Of course, the new owners wanted to sell the properties, but there were few buyers and, then unoccupied, the farm buildings slowly deteriorated.

To keep that deterioration (and the allied probability of depredation) to a minimum, the land was always "posted" by the new owners. The local sheriffs, thankful for insurance company and banker contributions to their re-election efforts, were more than happy to patrol the properties and drive off all trespassers – be they hobos seeking shelter in falling down farm houses or reasonably respectable characters like Calhoun Peabody.

Calhoun freely admitted he had disappointed Great Aunt Aurora by entering a trade. There was a valid reason for his decision to become what Great Aunt Aurora called "a common dealer in real estate". As a realtor, Uncle Calhoun was able to convince the banks and insurance companies to allow him unlimited access to their foreclosed properties in order to show them to prospective buyers.

Calhoun Peabody was wily. He had an ulterior motive. He was a dedicated, confirmed, and inveterate quail hunter. Those abandoned farms held great coveys of quail and Uncle Calhoun often walked the fields - accompanied not by a prospective buyer, but by an English Setter named George III and a twenty gauge shotgun loaded with 7 1/2 chill shot.

When he first visited Uncle Calhoun, Nathaniel Peabody was a rebellious and irresponsible young man, completely disinterested in his family's social position, unable to manage his finances and without any direction to his life.

Under Uncle Calhoun's tutelage, Nathaniel remained a rebellious and irresponsible young man, completely disinterested in his family's social position and unable to manage his finances, but he developed a purpose - an unwavering interest that gave direction to his life. It was Uncle Calhoun who taught him about the joys of shotgun hunting in general and of quail hunting in particular. Like his uncle Calhoun, Nathaniel Peabody became a dedicated, confirmed, deceptive, cunning, tricky and inveterate bird hunter.

When the War started, Nathaniel joined the U S Army and, due to his fluency in the Spanish language (and, possibly through family reputation), he served as military attaché to a number of American Embassies scattered around the world. He retired only a few months before our senior partner, Mr. Robertson Smythe, invited me to lunch and gave me the assignment of preparing the William Henry Peabody Spendthrift Trust. Of course, the beneficiary of that Spendthrift Trust was Major Nathaniel Peabody.

Mr. Smythe instructed me to write the document in the strictest of terms with no possibility of any kind of alienation or prepayment of monthly remittances and, above all, a trust document so clearly written that it could not be challenged in court. I did so. Then the elder Peabody died.

My first meeting with Major Nathaniel Peabody, USA (ret.) was, I'm sure, a disappointment to him. He expected to receive a lump sum distribution from his father's substantial estate. As I recall it, the first time he entered my office he immediately inquired if a partial distribution (as he put it - "a mere pittance of say twenty-five or fifty thousand dollars") might be made before the final settlement of the estate. I told him he would receive no lump sum disbursement either before or after the final settlement of his father's estate and that he was the beneficiary of a Spendthrift Trust with quite definite terms.

When the Major recovered from the shock, he asked if a prepayment of a few month remittances might be made. Of course, I refused. I told him no prepayment of any kind could be made. I further advised him that the terms of the Trust document specifically directed the Trustee to give him a check on the first day of each month – and not a single second sooner.

Over the course of the next month, I received communications from two other Philadelphia law firms, each inquiring about the terms of the Peabody Spendthrift Trust. I sent them copies of the document and never officially heard from them again. Informally, both complimented me on the tight structure and clear wording of the document. However, I must admit I made one serious error in draftsmanship.

Peabody came to my office and made one more plea for a partial lump sum settlement. I denied his request. Then he asked for an early delivery of his next scheduled remittance. Again, I denied his request. I told him the terms of the Spendthrift Trust had to be strictly applied, without variation whatsoever. The Major repeated those words - "strictly applied, without variation whatsoever". He then pointedly mentioned the Trust provision that required the Trustee to deliver a monthly check to the Trust beneficiary.

Without another word, he turned and left my office.

I was thunderstruck. I sat for a moment in shocked silence. I picked up the Spendthrift Trust document, read it very carefully and immediately went to Mr. Robertson Smythe's office suite. I was concerned, but Mr. Smythe only smiled.

"You drafted the Trust Agreement," he said. "You are the Trustee. You have to live with its terms. The Major's interpretation is correct. You must personally deliver the Trust remittances to Peabody on the first day of the month. I'm sure you will handle it with your usual efficiency."

Then he smiled again and arose from behind his desk. It was his way of suggesting the interview was over and that I might want to leave his office. I left his office.

Since that date, Major Nathaniel Peabody and I have been joined at the hip – the place where he keeps his usually empty wallet. On the first day of every one of the following months, I have been required to personally deliver the Major's Trust remittances. I believe Peabody purposely arranges to be hunting on the first day of nearly every month. I believe he purposely arranges to be hunting in some God forsaken place like the Argentine Patagonia or the Canadian wilderness or the Nicaraguan out-back or Arkansas.

I am a city boy. Hunting dogs do not like me. I am afraid of them and they bark at me. I do not like the woods or the animals that live in them. I am afraid of wild bears and I am afraid of firearms. The thought of encountering a rattlesnake or a bear in the woods fills me with a panic terror and I am grateful for the strength of the sphincter muscles in my lower abdomen.

I became a lawyer to raise my standard of living. I expected to develop the life style of people who live in upper class suburbs, where they sometimes dress for dinner and can enjoy the advantages of urban culture. I didn't expect to find myself spending at least one day a month in the company of men dressed in old wool shirts or trying to sleep in a cabin smelling of wood smoke or freezing inside a tent, protected from midnight marauding, vicious animals by nothing more than a thin sheet of plastic.

I didn't expect to find myself saddled with the job of personally delivering the Major's Spendthrift Trust remittances on the first day of every month, regardless of the uncivilized bear or snake infested part of the world in which he might decide to find himself.

Mr. Robertson Smythe thinks it's funny.

Woodcock - 1

After giving me directions to get from the airport to the camp and reminding me (unnecessarily) that delivery of his Spendthrift Trust remittance was due in two days, Major Nathaniel Peabody left for northern Maine where he joined others intent upon pursuing the Ruffed Grouse. I arrived in the camp in the late afternoon of the last day of the month and found him and Doctor Carmichael seated at the cabin's kitchen/dining/poker table. I had barely enough time to unpack and, with some alarm, view the height and condition of the upper bunk that I would occupy when a third hunter entered the cabin.

I didn't know this man, but it was clear that he had only recently been infected with the bird hunting malady. His hunting gear was all brand new. He hadn't even removed the size identification tag stapled to the back of his still factory clean L. L. Bean hunting jacket. We all watched as the young man opened his game pouch and, obviously proud of his achievement, withdrew a handful of dead birds with long pointed beaks.

"Just look at these Woodcock," he proudly ordered. "I got four of them."

The reaction from Peabody and Carmichael was not what he expected. They mumbled "Oh dear" and "Good Heavens". Then they were silent and avoided looking directly into the hunter's eyes.

Confused, the young man said "I understand they are good

to eat." There was no response. "They are good to eat, aren't they?" he asked. Again, there was no response. He broke the silence with another question. "How would you cook them?" Clearly, the young man was in need of advice. It was Doctor Carmichael who undertook the task.

"Although they were often cooked with feathers attached in 17th century England," the doctor began, "some of that century's recipes for the preparation of Woodcock called for plucking, but not drawing the bird."

"Drawing?" the young man asked.

"Eviscerating," Carmichael answered.

"Eviscerating?" the young man asked.

"Gutting," Carmichael answered.

"Oh," the young man said and his eyes opened a bit wider. The possibility of cooking a bird without removing its feathers and internal organs had never occurred to him. Apparently he did not consider that prospect to be a happy one.

"After parboiling it with salt, pepper and ginger," the doctor continued, "the Woodcock would be baked."

"Guts and all?" the young man questioned, straightening up and wrinkling his noise as if he had experienced a close encounter with a vat of over-ripe Limburger cheese.

"Yes. The intestines and all other internal organs remained in their usual places," Doctor Carmichael confirmed, "but the bird was first larded and covered with sweet herbs." It was evident the addition of lard and sweet herbs was not enough to induce the young man to give serious thought to re-creating the 17th century method of baking Woodcock.

Doctor Carmichael disregarded his expression. "When you eat a woodcock prepared in accordance with that ancient recipe, ..." the doctor paused for a moment and decided not to say "guts". Instead he said: "...innards and all, don't eat the craw and don't look for a gizzard. The Woodcock doesn't have one. Feeding mostly on soft earthworms and the like," he continued, "the bird doesn't seem to need one."

"That's repulsive," the young man said. "Cooking a bird, feathers and all and then eating it when its intestines are filled with angleworms that haven't even been ground up by a gizzard! Surely, no one eats them that way today."

"In my humble opinion," Doctor Carmichael agreed, "anyone with a palate more delicate than that of a hungry hyena would turn and run if offered such a dish. The eating of un-eviscerated Woodcock is not tolerated in any civilized country. In France, however, where the old recipe, with minor variations, is still popular, I am told un-gutted Woodcock are considered to be a gourmet delight. The French are capable of all sorts of outrages."

"There have to be better ways to bake Woodcock," the young man persisted.

"There are, of course, many modern recipes that use only the breasts of Woodcock," Carmichael admitted. The young man brightened up perceptibly. "But," the doctor warned, "they call for such additions as wine, chicken soup, onion, garlic, dill, celery seed and the like. The purpose of adding such strong condiment, I am sure, is to remove the terribly strong liverish taste of the bird. However, I am unable to find a single recipe in which that objective has been achieved. If you insist on experimenting, I can recommend only one recipe."

"And that one is…?" the young man asked.

"To improve the taste of Woodcock, soak them in kerosene for three days and then throw them away," the doctor's answered. The young man looked confused. "You look confused," Carmichael said. "Let me explain it this way. You appear to be impressed by the intelligence of our hunting dogs?" It was a question, not a statement, and the young man vigorously nodded his head.

"You certainly must have noticed none of our dogs will retrieve a dead Woodcock. Dogs will hunt them and point them and find their highly camouflaged corpses hidden in the forest leaves, but very, very few of them will put a dead Woodcock in its mouth. Are you as smart as a hunting dog?"

"If they taste so bad, why do you shoot them?" the young man asked.

"A legitimate question, my boy," Carmichael said. "There are good reasons for such behavior. First, wing shooting that zigzag flyer is a challenge. I'm sure Dickens had the Woodcock in mind when he named one of his Oliver Twist characters 'the Artful Dodger'. Second, the dog has worked hard. His displays of joy and enthusiasm at successfully exposing the Woodcocks' hiding places are always obvious. If you don't put the bird in your game pouch, you will be showing contempt for the animal's excellent work. A gentleman will never disappoint a good bird dog.

"Of course, as soon as the dog returns to the hunt, your companions will expect you to heave the Woodcock as far into the bush as possible. I am told the hunters of Upper Michigan practice throwing facsimile Woodcock as part of their preparation for the autumnal hunting season."

It was apparent that Carmichael had no compunction against disappointing a neophyte bird hunter. The young man, now somewhat crestfallen, looked down at his prizes. Then he slowly nodded his head and, somewhat reluctantly said: "I suppose I should throw them away."

"Oh, no," Major Peabody quickly interjected. "Oh, no! Don't do that. It would be terribly wasteful. In spite of what Doc Carmichael tells you, if properly handled, those Woodcock can produce an excellent dinner."

Now I was confused. Peabody had often advised me: "Never, never, no, never ever try to eat a Woodcock".

* * * * *

I'll admit I accepted Major Peabody's dinner invitation with mixed feelings. On the one hand, his solemn promise and firm insistence that he provide the meal led me to believe I would not (as was customary) have to pay for the dinner. On the other hand, I suspected he might be trying to do me grave gustatory injury by feeding me Woodcock.

As we entered Bookbinder's two days later, the matre'd immediately ushered us to a table saying: "Mr. Devereaux is waiting for you." A small man with hair, thin and thinning, arose and extended a loosely gripping hand. He was all smiles and exclaimed "Ah, Major Peabody, so good to meet you and…" He looked at me, paused and finally finished the sentence with "… and you, too." Peabody had forgotten to introduce me, an oversight for which I am thankful.

As we sat, Devereaux was sincere when he said: "I can't thank you enough for giving me those wonderful Woodcock and that so very interesting 17th century recipe - and just in the nick of time, too. My Gourmet Club will be meeting at my apartment next week. I do hope you'll reconsider and join us. You may bring your friend," he added, eyeing me speculatively.

"Very kind of you, Devereaux," the Major answered. "I love Woodcock baked in the ancient way, but, as I told you, I'm so allergic to them that I'd break out into large orange and purple spots if I ever took so much as one tiny taste."

"And I must be in San Diego - all next week - and maybe the following week, too," I hastily added, finally understanding how the Major managed to get rid of the Woodcock and, at the same time, con some stranger into paying for his and my dinner at Bookbinders.

Yes, as the Major had told us, if properly handled, Woodcock can produce an excellent meal.

Fiction is Stranger than Truth

We were in a cabin on the First South Branch of the Oconto River. It was the last day of November. The deer hunting season had ended and it was legal for hunters to again carry a shotgun into the woods and look for Ruffed Grouse. I spent an uncomfortable night in that cabin, waiting for midnight when I could give Major Nathaniel Peabody his monthly Spendthrift Trust remittance.

It was cold. It was very cold. The bunk assigned to me was the furthest from a potbellied wood-burning stove and I knew it would somehow be completely out of the heating business when I experienced my regular early morning call of nature.

It has always been my desire and my plan to live in a nice condo in Philadelphia and, when Pennsylvania winters became unbearable, in a nice condo in Florida. Both places have central heating and air-conditioning. They are civilized. It has never been my desire or plan to be trapped into wearing heavy woolen clothing and, on the first day of each month, having to personally deliver Major Peabody's checks, regardless of whatever part of the uncivilized world in which he might decide to station himself.

I'll admit I was not a happy camper and I complained about the cold weather. I was immediately confronted by a chorus of "You don't know what cold is" from the assembled bird hunters. There followed a series of comments all beginning with … "I can remember when it was so cold that…" Some of those comments (like the one referring to a brass monkey) were so extreme I began to think they weren't telling me the truth.

Major Peabody, of course, joined in with the rest of them. He told me duck hunters will get up at four in the morning during those almost sunless December days, get into leaky skiffs, paddle through two foot waves that turn to ice when they run over the boat's deck and then, in sub-zero temperatures, sit for hours in a blind while gale force winds whistle around them, hoping a duck will fly past them.

That was simply too much for me. I could conceive of no one being that stupid. I gave the Major a look of mammoth disbelief and gave voice to the thought that he was not only stretching the truth, but treating it in a most Cavalier fashion. Peabody called me aside and quietly chastised me for hinting he had told an untruth.

"In hunting camps," he told me, "the truthfulness of a companion's statements should always receive the full benefit of the doubt. Even a man's lack of accurate memory or a possibly unintended misstatement," Peabody explained, "should be gently corrected, not referred to as a lie or be subjected to flat challenge. Such an act," he warned me, "would be considered as socially unacceptable within any closely knit fraternity of men who regularly hunt together."

"For instance," Peabody told me. "Steve - the fellow who owns the place – you've heard him say he makes the best Bloody Mary in the galaxy?" I agreed. "Yes," I said. "I've heard him say it more than once and I've heard the other men agree with him - many times."

"Since I am addicted to aged single malt," Peabody continued, "I don't drink Bloody Mary and am not a good judge of them, but I can tell you this. If you speak privately with each of the other hunters, you'll discover Steve is the only one who thinks he makes the best Bloody Mary in the galaxy. Nevertheless, no one will disagrees with him"

I saw the Major's point and began to appreciate the grouse camp etiquette he was explaining to me. "I see," I said. "I see. Steve's friends don't want to hurt his feelings, so they agree with him."

"Ahhh .... Something like that," was the Major's response.

(In point of fact, the Major didn't want to disabuse his attorney. He didn't want to tell him his companions publicly agreed that Steve made the best Bloody Mary only because Steve, upon hearing the compliment, would immediately make a batch of them and hand them to the hunters who wouldn't have to get up from their chairs and mix their own drinks.)

The conversations moved from the weather to other hunting experiences and Major Peabody rejoined his friends and reported an occurrence at a Maine grouse camp. He had been hunting near a stand of young spruce when a bird exploded from cover so close to him he almost dropped his 20 ga. The grouse was nearly out of range by the time he fired. It sailed on and disappeared into the trees.

"That certainly is a strange story," one of the Major's hunting friends observed "I suppose you're going to admit it was the only shot you missed during the entire year?"

Peabody paid no attention to the comment and went on with his tale. "It is a strange story and it becomes even more strange. I walked into that stand of spruce, shaking my head and trying to understand how I could have missed. Then I heard a sound coming from above me. Gentlemen, the grouse fell out of the tree. I hadn't missed. I hit it. The bird had enough strength to fly to the tree, but that was all. It died there and fell to my feet."

The other hunters were silent. They exchanged sidelong glances and wouldn't look into the Major's eyes. Then one of them spoke. "I believe you, Major," he said. "That very same thing happens to me three or four times every season." He paused before adding: "Only I'm not lucky enough to be standing anywhere near the tree when the bird falls out of it."

Then one of the old timers took his turn. "It's nice to be with people who can recognize the truth when it is told," he said. "It's a terrible thing when people don't believe you. Terrible. Yes, terrible." He paused and took a sip of his Bloody Mary. "You may not believe this, but about fifteen years ago I was accused of telling a fib. I'll never forget it. It is burned in my memory.

"The grouse cycle was on the down side and there weren't many birds around, but it was a nice October day. The woods were beautiful and it was a good day for a walk. I was hunting on one of those long-ago abandoned logging roads north of the Pine River. I hadn't seen a thing and then, at about ten in the morning, this bird jumped up in front of me. I busted it and it fell in the middle of the trail.

"I was going to retrieve it when I heard a wooshing sound right over my head. I looked up in time to see a red-tailed hawk heading straight toward my bird. He was gliding down with his talons stretched out in front of him. He meant to steal my grouse and I wasn't going to let him do it. He grabbed it just as I fired at him. Well, I missed and he sailed away with my bird.

"You can imagine my surprise when I saw a four point buck lying alongside the trail. He must have stuck his head out of the brush just as I shot at the hawk." He took another sip of his drink, and slowly moved his head from side to side. "I still can't believe it." he said. "The game warden didn't believe me. Neither did the judge. I was convicted of killing a deer out of season."

I could commiserate with the poor man as he sat there, slowly shaking his head in dismay. "It seems to me," I said, "the judicial system has treated you quite badly. I suppose there might have been some technical violation, but the judge should have recognized the basic equities of your situation. You were victimized by conditions entirely beyond your control. Had I been the judge, I would have rapped the gavel and said: Case dismissed in the interests of justice."

The old hunter nodded his head in agreement. "That's what I had hoped would happen, but I suppose the judge assigned too much weight to the fact that the deer was killed with double ought buckshot and not by seven and a half chill bird load."

Bear Story

Six grouse hunters were sharing a cabin near a small stream located deep in a sparsely populated area of Michigan's Upper Peninsula - the "UP" as it is universally called. Five of the men were from the U.P. (That accounts for their generic designation of "UP-ers" - a/k/a "Yoopers"). The sixth hunter was Major Nathaniel Peabody,

The men are friends of long standing. Each autumn, when the fallen leaves of maples and hardwoods turn the forest floor earth colored, they meet in the Upper Peninsula to hunt Ruffed Grouse and Woodcock. Their relationship is such that Peabody has been officially designated an Honorary Yooper, a title seldom granted to flatlanders.

There are infinitely more hunters and fishermen per square yard in the UP than anywhere else in the Republic. By and large, Yoopers have not been regimented by urban life style and the Major harbors a sincere affection for each of his Yooper hunting companions. They return the favor. When in their camp, Peabody has but once to rattle the ice cubes in an empty glass and it is immediately re-filled.

Long before the armed services popularized the rule: "Don't ask - Don't tell", it has been in effect in the UP. If venison is served during a Yooper grouse camp - a week or so before the opening of deer season - it is considered to be a social faux pas for anyone to inquire into the date when the deer may have been killed. It is considered to be insanity for anyone to truthfully answer such a question. Major Peabody always enjoyed the venison dinners without showing interest in the age of the meat.

Is it impossible to over-estimate the importance of deer season in the UP. Killing a buck is a prerequisite to the right to vote. When the deer hunting season begins, it seems like everyone heads for the woods. Businesses hang out "Closed" signs. Factories lay empty, abandoned by their employees. Any boy able to carry a 30/30 skips school. Court calendars are clear because all the UP lawyers are hunting deer instead of clients. If an out-of-state attorney comes into a UP town, he will find no local attorneys to fight with. If two foreign lawyers come into a UP town to do legal battle, they must wait patiently until the judge returns from his deer camp and opens court.

The dinner at the Major's UP grouse camp celebrated the fact that in only another nineteen days, the deer season would be officially open. The enthusiastic dinner table conversation was, therefore, limited to the plans for hunt preparations and tales of past deer season happenings. The same subject matter overwhelmed the conversations during the dish washing and continued well into the social hour(s) that followed.

Peabody was not his usual garrulous self. He is not a deer hunter. While he is not averse to the practice, his interest in the sport is modest. He listened politely to the stories and talk surrounding him, occasionally rattling his ice cubes and, even less occasionally, offering comments like: "That's funny," "You don't say?" and "Amazing!"

(When the word, "Amazing" is often used in the UP. Every one knows it is the translation into printable English of a common Yooper two word expression that describes the by-product of a male cow. When the word 'amazing' is used by someone listening to a Yooper's story, it is an acceptable way to emphatically signify utter and complete disbelief.)

The rare occurrence of a quiet Major Nathaniel Peabody attracted the attention of one of his Yooper friends. "Peabody, are you sick?" he asked. "Oh, no," another Yooper answered before the Major could say a word. "The Major is only interested in birds. If deer flew, he'd be up here with us every November. He's a shot gunner. You may not believe this. Major Peabody doesn't own a deer rifle – not even one."

A chorus of expressions of disbelief followed that last revelation.

"Amazing!"

"It can't be true!"

"Peabody not owning a deer rifle? I don't believe it!"

Peabody looked at the smirking faces of his companions and knew it was time for him to defend himself. "It isn't necessary to carry one of your outsized canons to finish off a large quadruped," he said.

"Amazing," one of his fellow hunters emphatically exclaimed.

"No," Peabody countered. "Not 'amazing' at all. It's the truth."

"Amazing," another of his friends repeated.

Peabody slowly shook his head in feigned disbelief. "Gentlemen," he said, "I fear you have neglected your studies of history. There was a time when gunpowder was unknown in the entire world. Later, it was known only in China where, incidentally, it was used exclusively to make fireworks. In those days, people did not have deer rifles and yet the meat of large wild animals formed a part of their regular diet."

Peabody leaned back in his chair, rattled the ice in his empty glass and wondered what he as going to say next. While refreshing the Major's libation, his host entered the argument. "Back in those days, doctors used leeches and bleeding to cure sickness. Nowadays the medics use more advanced methods.

It's the same with hunters. We have no need to use primitive, inefficient and ineffective hunting methods - hence the present-day, beautiful deer rifle. The process is called 'the advancement of civilization'."

Another of the Yoopers took up the cudgel. "You may not need a rifle to protect yourself from deer. They'll run away. But suppose you're picking berries and you run into a bear. Then what could you do without appropriate modern rifled weaponry?"

Peabody was ready. "Strange you should ask," he said. "That very thing happened to me a few years ago right here in Iron County. I was grouse hunting and ran into a nice patch of raspberries. I began to fill my hat when a black bear the size of the Empire State Building reared up in front of me and let go with a snarl that would have frightened the living bejaysus out of Ivan the Terrible. I decided that shooting the beast with 7 1/2 chilled shot was not the prudent thing to do. It would have made him angrier and he was already quite mad at me for invading his berry patch.

"I'm sure you are all aware of the term 'running down a deer'?" It was a question. Two of the Yoopers slowly nodded while the three younger men looked perplexed.

"The pre-gun-weapon-era Indians," the Major explained, "would chase a deer on foot. They would stay on its trail exerting constant pressure until the animal dropped from exhaustion." The young men looked to the older ones for confirmation and saw them give affirmative nods. Not one of them said 'amazing'.

"I jumped up and down," Peabody said. "I waved my arms and shouted the most blood curdling yells I could imagine. The bear began to run at full speed. I immediately dropped the shotgun as unnecessary baggage and joined in the race. A bear can sprint at high speed for short distances, but it isn't able to maintain that pace for very long. My bear had the best of it for the first four or five rods. Then I began to gain on him.

"The bear apparently led a life even more dissolute than my own. After some ten minutes, it began to slow down. Of course, the bear had prepared for winter hibernation and had developed a thick layer of fat. That extra weight combined with the effects of the heat of the day and the bear's thick fur coat took their toll.

"The race led us over a large fallen log and half way up a steep wooded hill. Not more than ten feet separated me from the beast when it faltered, sunk to the ground, gasped, and died on the spot. I had run that bear to death.

"Frankly, friends," Peabody continued, "I'll admit I, too, was approaching exhaustion. If that creature had been able to run for a few more minutes, I would have collapsed and the bear would have caught up with me and eaten me."

In unison, the five Yoopers spoke. "Amazing," they said.

Experts

"You don't appear to be in a jovial mood," I said to Major Peabody, "Do I note a touch of discontent?"

The Major didn't bother to answer. He favored me with an angry, sullen, threatening stare. We were in my apartment, waiting for the lovely Stephanie. She had invited us to an afternoon reception honoring the author of the book, "How to Live to be a Hundred and Ten". The man, she said, was internationally recognized as an expert in matters of diet and health.

I knew how much Peabody hated afternoon social affairs. He would rather be tortured by the Mescalero Apache and staked out over a hill of fire ants. If he dislikes anything more than cocktail parties, it is writers and their elephantine egos, but he was trapped. He would never disappoint the lovely Stephanie. Years ago she invited him to a performance of Swan Lake. Peabody seriously considered contracting anthrax or, alternatively, committing suicide. However, he went to the ballet rather than disappoint her.

And so, to avoid disappointing her, the Major felt compelled to spend an afternoon in the presence of not only an author, but an expert, to boot. The Major's opinion of so-called experts was lower than his opinion of politicians.

Though Peabody detested television, while we waited for the lovely Stephanie to arrive, we watched a panel of TV newscasters interviewing an expert on military matters. "Will you listen to those fools." Peabody exclaimed. "Experts? Hah!

We are besieged and bedeviled by armies of so-called experts. I blame it on the television news programs. They have to fill their time slot with something so they hire some photogenic ex-officer who was probably cashiered for incompetence ten years ago. They call him an 'expert' and he proceeds to tell everyone how run the war in Timbuktu. Expert? My foot." (The Major didn't say "foot". He mentioned a different part of his anatomy)

"Hollywood types," he continued, "are excellent examples of experts. Some high school dropout with a low pitched voice, a reasonably straight nose and an outsized bust makes a few million dollars as an actress. Then, magically, she becomes an expert on everything. She's on the talk shows confidently telling us how to save the universe from whatever threat has most recently been imagined by other experts. Damn experts, damn television and damn me for watching it." The Major went to the television set and punched the OFF button with such vigor. I thought he might break his trigger finger.

"Young man," he said to me, "I am indebted to your legal profession." That statement came as a complete surprise to me. I know the Major's low opinion of attorneys. I'm afraid my jaw dropped. "Yes, lawyers have properly defined the true value of an expert's opinion." Peabody's explanatory statement did nothing to cause a change in my expression. Apparently, Peabody noticed my confusion and decided to offer clarification.

"Let's say Uncle Pete dies at the ripe old age of 85," he said. "He wills his entire estate to the young, nicely sculptured blonde who lives next door. Uncle Pete's only living blood relative tries to break the will. He goes to an attorney who proceeds to hire three psychiatrists who testify as expert witnesses. Each one swears that Uncle Pete must have been operating under undue influence and was incompetent when the will was signed.

"The young, nicely sculptured blonde's attorney promptly puts three other psychiatrists on the stand. His experts all testify that Uncle Pete's association with the young blonde proved he was not only lucky, but unquestionably sane. Each set of expert witnesses testifies the other one doesn't know what they're talking about.

"The legal profession has performed a great service to the discerning public. Lawyers - bless their souls - have shown both sets of experts are incompetent. Their cross examination of the other guy's expert witness proves no one should believe any of them."

The toot-toot-toot of a horn announced the lovely Stephanie's arrival. Peabody disguised his unhappiness and was reasonably pleasant on the trip to the country home of the hostess. She met us at the door and we were introduced to the author - the guest of honor - the expert on health and longevity. The man wore a tweedy jacket, a tattersall shirt and a bow tie - the disguise regularly worn by those trying to fool the public into believing they are intellectual.

As usual, Major Peabody searched the room for anyone who looked like he might be a bird hunter. He was disappointed. Finding none, he stuck close to me for protection. He puppy dogged behind me with a disregarded glass of white wine in his hand. He forced smiles and occasionally used up two or three sentences before he could escape an unwanted conversation.

The Major's ability to be civil when under the pressure of trying circumstances is limited to, at best, no more than two hours. Two and a half hours had already passed when the hostess led the writer toward us. Five or six ready-to-gush females and an equal number of sycophant males trailed in his wake.

"I see you are quite tanned Major," the guest of honor observed. "Do you spend much time in the sun?"

"As much time in the un-crowded out-of-doors as I possibly can," was Peabody's terse response. I believe I was the only one who understood why he emphasized the word 'un-crowded'. He desperately wanted to get away from the cocktail party. The author was secretly hoping for the answer the Major gave. Now he had another opportunity to display his wisdom. "Oh my! The sun can be quite dangerous, Major Peabody. You do use sun screen?"

"No. I can't be bothered with it. I tried it once, but I sweat. The stuff ran into my eyes and I couldn't shoot straight."

"You should avoid the risk of developing skin cancer, Major," the expert seriously intoned. The retinue congregating around him quickly nodded in agreement. "It's almost as dangerous as eating red meat," one of them said, trying to adopt the expert's same serious intonation. "Or any meat," another one added.

"Surely, you don't eat meat, Major," the author said, but when his eyes met Peabody's stern and unwavering stare, he had reason to question the assumption. "You don't. Do you?" he questioned.

"Grouse and duck," Peabody immediately answered. Then he paused for a moment and, for the benefit of the expert and his retinue, gave a more complete response. "Canvasback, Mallard and Teal are very good. So is pheasant. Occasionally one of my hunting companions will provide me with venison or elk or antelope. When they neglect me, I'm reduced to eating Porterhouse steak or rack of lamb. I like ham, too - and any kind of pork - roasts, chops, bacon - all very tasty."

Consternation! Surprise! An audible gasp came from both the author and the obsequious group surrounding him. "Major! I feel it is incumbent upon me to beg you to change your unhealthy patterns. If you will follow my wholesome dietary and hygienic rules, a long and active life lies in front of you. If not, well..."

Again, heads nodded in agreement. They needed to wait only seconds before the Major responded.

"I will bet one thousand dollars that I will live longer than you." Sounds like: "Oh, come now" and "Well - well" and "I see" came from the author as he backed away and his shocked entourage retreated in confusion. As gracefully as she could, Stephanie told the hostess she really had to return to Philadelphia to attend a non-existent meeting of the Friends of the Philharmonic. She quickly whisked us away.

On the trip back to the city, Stephanie, at first, was silent. After a few miles she smiled. A few miles later, finally, she chuckled. She couldn't help but ask the Major what he would have done if the man had accepted his bet.

"It is and continues to be my belief," Peabody told her, "that all experts publicly exude absolute confidence in their opinions. However, when it comes to putting their money where their mouths are, that confidence disappears and they show a strange but entirely understandable reluctance to 'put up'."

"But, what if he took your bet," she persisted

"I wasn't worried," he answered. "I was just trying to shut him up. Suppose he made the bet and suppose he won. He'd have a hard time collecting from me."

Dog's Best Friend

Major Peabody invited his apartment building's Resident Agent into his quarters and did his best to engage him in pleasant conversation. It was soon apparent that the man had no time for small talk. He looked at the Major through narrowing and suspicious eyes. His interest was limited. He wanted to know only if something in the apartment had stopped working and needed repair.

Peabody responded by mentioning his long residence and cordial relations with the management of the corporation that owned the apartment complex. The agent was suspicious. He guessed at the Major's purpose and volunteered the information that rent reductions were completely out of the question.

Peabody confused him by saying such a thought never occurred to him and offered to provide a cigar and a dollop of appropriately aged, single malt Scotch whisky. When the agent refused the offer, Peabody knew he faced an uphill battle, but he persevered.

"I believe I saw Mrs. Johnson bring a bag of kitty litter into the elevator last week," the Major said, "and, if I'm not mistaken, for some years now I've heard a canary sing from one of the upper apartments. I enjoy the cheerful chirping of that lovely canary. I love birds and kitty cats, too – in fact, any kind of animals."

Before he could continue, the agent cut to the chase. "Aha." he cried out. "Now I know what you're after. It won't work,

Major."

Disregarding the agent's unequivocal statement and stony expression, Peabody pressed onward. "Only a wise and highly intelligence person is able to recognize the value of disregarding counterproductive and insane lease provisions," he said. "You, for example, have winked at the lease provisions that say 'No Pets'. What can be wrong with letting a lonely old woman keep a canary or a cat? I compliment you on your so very good judgment."

The Agent abruptly arose from the chair. "We've already been over this, Major Peabody," he said over his shoulder as he walked toward the door. "Cats and birds are one thing. Dogs are another. The company policy is: NO DOGS - and NO DOGS it is. Not a little tiny Chihuahua. Not a huge, ugly, barking hound of the Baskervilles like the one you smuggled in here. I gave you three days to get rid of it. You have one day left. If that monstrosity is still here, prepare yourself for an eviction notice!" He made his escape and slammed the door.

As soon as it heard the door shut and knew it was safe to make an appearance, a dog came from his hiding place in the Major's bedroom. Alexander the Great was a wire-haired, pointing Griffon. Born in northern Minnesota, the dog was trained to find and hold Ruffed Grouse, He was trained well. Peabody had often hunted over Alexander and was impressed by the animal's abilities.

Recently, Alexander's owner died after struggling with a heart that just wouldn't behave. His Testament bequeathed the animal to the Major. Peabody couldn't keep Alexander in his apartment and he soon discovered finding a Philadelphia home for the dog was not an easy task. Few people shared his love of hunting dogs. Man's inhumanity to dog was more widespread than can be imagined.

Damnit all, anyway, the Major thought. There has to be a

way around this. He considered possible alternatives. He could murder that stubborn, unfair scoundrel - the Resident Agent - and hope the replacement would be more amenable to reason. He discarded that thought for the obvious reason. The possibility of the company sending a reasonable man to replace a murdered building manager was miniscule.

It occurred to him he could move to another apartment where the landlord didn't mind a dog pen in the building's back lot, didn't mind circles of dead grass where the chemicals in dog by-product made growth of grass impossible for years and didn't mind dog hair and dog smell in and around a tenant's quarters.

No, the Major concluded, it would be impossible to find such a landlord in Philadelphia. He recalled his long ago attempts to convince his own wife of the gratifying enjoyment of association with hunting dogs. She reacted by citing the presence of his Labrador Retriever as a basis for the cruel and inhuman treatment she alleged in her divorce complaint. Her attorney had a hard time convincing her not to name the dog as a co-respondent.

Peabody thought about again trying to talk his attorney into providing a home for Alexander the Great. It was a good plan, but there were two problems. The attorney knew nothing about dogs. It wouldn't take a year before Alexander would have been pampered to such an extent that it would be little more than a house pet, unwilling or unable to do the work of a hunting dog. The second problem was more serious. The lawyer had flatly refused the proposition and, worse, he had already convinced the lovely Stephanie to reject any dog sitting proposition the Major might advance to her.

"Well," Peabody said as he scratched the head Alexander had conveniently laid in his lap, "I suppose I can call the animal shelter. They might find a good home for you."

Alexander heard and understood. He lifted his head and looked alarmed. Suppose, the dog thought, they place me with some non-hunter. Suppose they give me to a gun controller. I might never hunt grouse again. The Major watched as tears began to form in Alexander's eyes.

An equally terrible scenario occurred to the Major. A wire-haired Griffon is much too big to be a lap dog. It is not a handsome animal and few, if any, would go so far as to call it cute. A Griffon is not the kind of dog taken from animal shelters and given to children as pets. Suppose, the Major thought, the animal shelter couldn't find anyone to take Alexander. They'd push him into a vacuum tank and suck the air out. Alexander's last moments on earth would be terrible.

Time was running out and one by one the Major's options were disappearing. In desperation, he called his friend, Doc Carmichael. "I've got a tough problem and I need your help, Doc," he said. "I'm quite depressed and I don't know where to turn. I'm beginning to think euthanasia is the only solution left."

"I can't become directly involved," was Carmichael's immediate response. "The stupid laws being as they are, I could be charged with murder. I'll give you a note identifying the chemicals you'll need and the formula for preparing a dosage. Then you're on your own. The product is lethal. It will do the job quickly. You won't suffer much."

"It's not for me, you idiot," Peabody answered. "It's for a dog."

An hour later, Carmichael arrived at the Major's apartment carrying the proverbial doctor's little black bag. It contained a hypodermic needle and a mixture of drugs calculated to propel a 65 pound dog into a painless but permanent sleep.

* * * * *

Alexander lay quietly in the backseat of the Jeep, his muzzle resting on his paws. He seemed to mirror the sadness of the two men who sat in gray, dejected silence as they drove to Carmichael's cottage where Alexander the Great's final resting place would overlook a tree lined lake.

It seemed obvious that Alexander knew what was in store for him. Through pleading eyes, he watched as Doc Carmichael opened his little black bag.

* * * * *

"I need a drink," the Major announced when he returned to his apartment. "So do I" said a solemn and worried Doc Carmichael. "I'm not happy with what happened at the lake. How am I ever going to explain it to Janell?"

Peabody consoled him. "She won't blame you for refusing to kill an animal and in time she'll get to love Alexander. She'll overlook the hair on the furniture. Look at the bright side, Doc. Now we can both hunt over a great Ruffed Grouse dog."

"Yes," Carmichael agreed, "but I'm the one who has to feed him and pay the veterinary bills."

Peabody merely smiled.

Animal Rights

Major Nathaniel Peabody does not enjoy cocktail parties. During the years he served as a Military Attaché in various United States embassies, it was his duty to attend them. He was forced to hold a martini in his hand (without drinking it) for entire Saturday afternoons when he would have preferred to be in the field, hunting the local waterfowl and upland birds.

Moreover, as he matured the Major developed a distaste (which eventually approached a loathing) for small talk that does not concern itself with dogs or shotguns. Peabody considers attending cocktail parties to be an activity only slightly less offensive than stealing pennies from the eyes of the dead.

When he retired and established his residence in Philadelphia, Major Peabody immediately took a fancy to my fiancé. Though she is some thirty years his junior and, like me, definitely not the outdoor type, the lovely Stephanie charmed him. She is the only one who can induce him to attend a Main Line cocktail party and has done so on more than one occasion. And so, as a result of Stephanie's cajoling, Major Peabody agreed to accompany us to such an affair.

There are people in the suburbs surrounding Philadelphia who have deep commitments to (but little understanding of) the environment, animal rights and other "feel good" movements. Whenever a hostess informs her guests of the Major's out-of-doors activities, he is, he says, confronted by aggressive women in flat heeled shoes and tweedy, delicate men who engage him in argument or attempt to secure his approval of some distasteful theory.

Peabody regularly extracts himself from such situations by brutally ending all conversations. He has become an expert at it. For example, a lady author showed no interest in a then current newspaper headline about a woman who murdered her husband with an axe. She casually dismissed the story with the words "he probably drove her to it." However, when someone mentioned how a Bryn Mawr man cut off his wife's head, the woman went ballistic in her outrage.

If the lady had directed equal anger toward the woman who murdered her husband, the Major would have remained silent. However, the lady's selective outrage offended him. Peabody successfully terminated her diatribe with a single sentence. When he commented: "She probably was too tall, anyway," silence occurred abruptly and the author and her coterie of sycophants slowly backed away.

Peabody's ploy to avoid what he considers to be ridiculous chatter has been remarkably effective. When a lady advocate of gun control gushed about the two fawns that regularly visited her back yard, the Major brightened up and offered to get a gun and shoot them both. In answer to the question: "Major Peabody, how can you shoot those beautiful pheasants?" he says: "I like to kill things."

On this occasion, the party was in full swing and the lovely Stephanie was mingling. I watched the Major as he stood alone, tried (unsuccessfully) not to appear to be bored and, at short intervals, looked at his wrist watch. I went to keep him company. Our hostess had the same purpose and we simultaneously arrived at his side.

"You're Major Peabody, aren't you," she began.

"Guilty," he answered

"What a delight to meet you. I've heard so much about

you."

"Mmmmmm," was his response.

"You spend so much time communing with nature and with her wild creatures. I know you're a hunter, but don't you really believe animals merit our protection and should have rights, just as human beings have rights?"

"I used to dismiss the Animal Rights people as purveyors of anthropomorphic, metaphysical nonsense," the Major said and his hostess began to look alarmed. He continued: "At first, I was sure such people had undergone brain surgery and the surgeon didn't put everything back, but now I have reason to re-visit that conclusion. There may be something to Animal Rights after all."

The hostess regained her composure and looked pleased. I couldn't believe my ears. The Major was definitely not under the influence of single malt Scotch whisky. I could think of nothing else that might cause him to make such an uncharacteristic statement. Certainly anyone who knew him would have been stunned. I was so surprised I involuntarily exclaimed: "Oh?"

"You seem surprised, my boy," said the Major. "Can it be possible you consider me to be an unreconstructed realist, congenitally unable to give lip service to positions maintained by people who have never worn out a pair of boots in their entire lives and wouldn't recognize Mother Nature if she knocked them down and sat on them."

"Yes," I admitted, as our hostess again began to look disturbed.

Peabody smiled at her and went on: "Please be assured," he said to her, "not a single matter involving the environment and the out-of-doors escapes my attention and careful consideration. Take this matter of Animal Rights, for example. Our Founding Fathers declared all men to be created equal and endowed with certain inalienable rights, including life, liberty and the pursuit of happiness. The Animal Rights folks claim these constitutional guarantees should be extended not only to men, but also to women and other animals."

His statement was reassuring, but the last phrase did nothing to completely erase our hostess' anxiety. The Major's sincerity and his next words led her to volunteer another cautious smile.

"I'm willing to wholeheartedly accept your suggestion to recognize Animal Rights", Peabody said as he maneuvered her into a corner where she could not escape. "As much as I applaud your efforts," the Major added, "I don't believe Animal Rights advocates have addressed a matter that should concern us all. If animals are to have rights, they must also have responsibilities." A look of uncertainty re-appeared on the hostess' face.

Major Peabody smiled at his hostess and said: "I have seen groups of your friends carrying signs and railing against Canadians who, in accordance with their government's regulations, harvest seals. Polar Bears eat seals. I've seen no one carrying signs on the frozen tundra or picketing a Royal Canadian Mounted Police station, insisting they take Polar Bears into custody and prosecute them for murder and cannibalism.

"Geese trespass on farmers' posted fields. They steal corn and grain and fly off to protected sanctuaries where the Constable cannot serve them with papers hailing them into court and requiring them to defend themselves against charges of criminal trespass and felony theft. There is no attempt to make them pay civil damages for their depredations.

"Moreover geese leave their calling cards on golf courses, in parks and on lawns surrounding waterways. If you were to perform their very same acts, the police would be after you in a minute. To my knowledge, not a single goose has ever been charged with indecent behavior or littering.

"If a teacher gives some schoolboy a well deserved backhander, the School Board and the public at large call it Child Abuse and will have her hide. Female gorillas steal simian babies, fish eat fry, male black bear, if given a chance, will kill their young. Nevertheless, child abuse in the animal kingdom goes unpunished.

"I believe in Equal Justice. I believe animal wrongdoers should be subject to the same fines and prison terms that are meted out to human criminals. If you are to have any credibility at all, your proposals to give rights to animals must contain provisions requiring the animals to assume responsibilities. You must provide for regulations to bring animal malefactors to justice.

"I will happily volunteer to work with your Legislation Committee to draft appropriate terminology for an Animal Responsibility law. Please ask the committeepersons to tell me the dates and times of their next meetings and I will arrange my schedule, but, I must inform you now, I believe in the death penalty."

A bewildered hostess edged out of the corner, mumbled something about "How very interesting", and fled.

At the end of the month when I delivered the Major's Spendthrift Trust remittance, he recalled the conversation. "Can you believe it?" he said. "In spite of my generous offer to assist them, no one ever contacted me. It must have been my support of the death penalty."

It's Hell to Grow Old

Jerry Olsen owns hunting land deep in the Maine woods. The land contains a cabin. The cabin contains a wood stove and Coleman lanterns because it is far from electricity and propane gas services. The building consists of one large room with enough double bunks to sleep six – twelve if everyone is real friendly. The walls are decorated with pictures from long out-of-date calendars, horns and a few poorly mounted birds and fish. On a sunny day it might be possible to see through the windows. The floor is covered with linoleum that showed wear and tear twelve years ago. There is nothing inside the cabin that would tempt a thief.

I know about that cabin. Three years ago I spent two nights there. I intended to spend only one, but when I tried to leave on the morning of the second day, I became so hopelessly lost in the maze of abandoned, muddy, two rut logging roads that I believe it was only by the intervention of a Divine Providence that I managed to find my way back to the cabin before the sun had set and I was left alone in the dark, surrounded by vicious wild beasts.

This was my second visit to Jerry Olsen's cabin in the woods. Mr. Olsen had invited Major Peabody, Doctor Carmichael and two others to join him to participate in what he called The Seventeenth Annual Lying and Opening Day Ruffed Grouse Hunting Competition. He always invited four hunters because he didn't consider it to be poker unless there were at least five people at the table. The Major and Doc

39

Carmichael always participated in the annual competitions, but there is no guarantee that anyone will be re-invited. If a hunter behaves badly or ground swats a bird, he is blacklisted forever.

I was again in attendance, not because I was invited, but because the first day of the month occurred in the middle of the planned hunt and I was obliged to deliver the Major's Spendthrift Trust remittance on that day. This time I had the foresight to demand a detailed map showing the way from cabin to county road. I did not appreciate the little explanatory notes that Mr. Olsen added to his hand drawn map. Notes like: LOOKOUT - Bear Den Here, and BE CAREFUL - Watch for Wolverines and Poisonous Snakes.

When I arrived at the camp, I expected to find Major Peabody in his usual end-of-month destitute situation. I was surprised to find him enjoying an unaccustomed state of relatively robust finance. However, due to a number of second-best poker hands, the Major was broke before the evening ended. Jerry Olsen, Doctor Carmichael and the other two hunters, particularly the young man called Lefty, were all smiling and jovial.

The Major, however, was understandably depressed. He grumbled. He left the table. He had a Scotch and water. He punctuated his sips with crotchety comment. Then he retired to his bunk. He was in such a foul mood he didn't even smile when, at the stroke of midnight, I delivered his monthly remittance. He merely snorted, took the envelope from my hand and crammed it beneath his pillow.

The next morning, Mr. Olsen prepared breakfast. A ten pound bag of yellow onions lay on the kitchen counter beside him. He was dicing one of them. "Lefty," he ordered, "get me some potatoes for the raw fries and find a green pepper, too."

Lefty heaved a large Styrofoam ice chest onto the table. The top half of the chest held the perishable food. Lefty found a pepper and tossed it to Mr. Olsen. "I suppose we need all this ice for libations," he said, "but it sure makes this thing hard to lift." He took the chest from the table and returned it to the floor. Then he picked up the twenty pound bag of potatoes. "These potatoes are heavy," he complained, hoisting them onto the counter. "Are you trying to give me a hernia?" he asked

Doc Carmichael sat on the edge of a lower bunk and laced his Chippewa's. He was listening to them. "Relax Lefty," he said. "You have nothing to worry about. If you had to carry my game bag, by the end of the day the strain might rupture you, but you don't shoot that well. Your game bag is never that heavy. You won't ever run the risk of a hernia."

Major Peabody had already finished dressing. From the look on his face, I was sure he was still upset by his reverses at the poker table. His tone of voice confirmed my suspicion. "That's the trouble with you youngsters," he muttered. "You don't keep yourselves in shape. When I was your age I could easily lift my own weight."

"When you were my age," Lefty answered, "I wasn't even born. That's the trouble with you old timers. Your mind plays tricks on you. Memory loss, you know. Lift your own weight? Hah! It won't be long before you'll have trouble lifting a Scotch and water."

Peabody reacted immediately. It was clear that he was still upset by his bad luck at cards. Lefty's taunt added insult to that injury. Obviously, the Major was also annoyed when Lefty called him an "old timer". Peabody would never admit that he had lost any of his prowess or was not in the prime of his life.

"Don't get snotty, Lefty," he said. "I'm in better shape than you are."

I recognized what was going on. My area of legal expertise includes estate planning. I draft a lot of Testamentary Trusts for old people. When the aging process accelerates and the wheels begin to come off – especially with men who have led active lives – any suggestion of impairment of their physical abilities is often strenuously denied, even when the effects of age are obvious to everyone.

I didn't want to see Peabody agitated by any further insensitive remarks from Lefty. I knew the Major would consider them to be a challenge. They might provoke him into saying something he would later regret. I thought it was time to change the subject. "Well, well, well," I said as I slid down from one of the top bunks. "Looks like bacon, eggs and raw fries for breakfast. That ought to fill us up. Are you ready to shoot some birds, Major?"

Peabody disregarded my question. "That'll be the day, you young pup," he said to Lefty, walking toward him in a nearly threatening manner. "Unlike you, I'm in excellent condition. I've always watched my diet, exercised regularly and taken good care of my body." That last statement came as such a surprise to Doctor Carmichael that he inadvertently raised his eyebrows, gave a sidelong glance in the Major's direction and then shook his head in disbelief.

"Just look at you," Peabody continued. "Years of drinking Canadian whiskies and other similar unspeakable dissipations have reduced you to such a condition that you can hardly lift a twenty pound bag of potatoes from floor to table. I could life that bag with one hand."

Lefty said: "Hah!"

"And that onion bag, too," Peabody added in response, "both in the same hand." He paused for not more than a second before adding: "I could hold them out straight in front of me."

"Now, Major," I soothed. "No need to carry on. Lefty didn't mean anything. He was just kidding."

"You, too?" the Major said, turning to me, "you, too? You think I can't do it? I'm not kidding. I'll bet anyone fifty dollars

I can take both bags in one hand and hold them out in front of me for a full minute – no, for five minutes - without dropping them."

Peabody's companions looked at each other.

"OK", Lefty said. "You've got a bet."

"I want in, too," Jerry Olsen said.

"Me, too," said the fourth hunter who was still lying in his bunk.

"Damn right," was Peabody's answer. "I can do it." He looked at Carmichael. "I suppose you want a piece of it, Doc? Don't be bashful." Carmichael wasn't a bit reluctant. Over the years, he had lost plenty on bets with the Major. He was eager to get a bit of it back. I thought it was a good time for me to get in on the bet, too.

Major Peabody dumped the potatoes and the onions onto the table, took the two empty bags in his right hand and held them out in front of him. "Do you want to begin the timing?" he asked Doc Carmichael.

Shame

"Shame on you, sir. Shame on you," Jerry Olsen said to Major Peabody. Jerry opened his wallet and removed fifty dollars. "I consider your actions to be reprehensible," he said as he handed the bills to the Major.

Peabody smiled and moved his extended palm-up hand to me, to Lefty, to the fourth hunter and, finally, to Doctor Carmichael. We all contributed to the stack of bills that filled his hand. "I won't bother to count the money," the Major said. "Such an act would suggest that I didn't trust you to accurately pay your honest obligations."

Peabody sat down at the table and moved some of the breakfast dishes to make space. Then, aloud and one by one, he carefully counted the bills. "Ten, twenty, thirty, ..."

"Honest obligation! Honest obligations," Lefty loudly exclaimed. "This is incredible. Will you listen to the nerve of the man? There's nothing honest about chicanery and deceit, Major. You've taken advantage of our simple innocence. The least you can do is blush."

"Blush?" Doc Carmichael asked in amazement. "Peabody is shameless. He hasn't blushed in his entire life."

The Major carefully folded the bills and shoved them into the breast pocket of his wool shirt. "Come now gentlemen," he said. "It was greed, pure greed that motivated you to take the bet. You are, each one of you, about as innocent as a Chicago Alderman. You took the bet because you thought you could take advantage of me, a helpless and naïve boy from the country."

"I can't take much more of this," Lefty said. "Please ask him to stop, Doc. I'm just about ready to throw up."

Major Peabody merely smiled, tapped the pocket where the two hundred and fifty dollars safely resided and, ignoring the dismay of his friends, returned to his theme. "Last night at the poker table, all four of you treated me in a most unconscionable manner. You dealt me second best hands all evening. It is gratifying to see that the Fates have now evened the score and," he paused as he favored his companions with a broad smile, "decided to add an appropriate surcharge to compensate me for having to spend the evening suffering through your insulting commentaries."

Jerry slowly shook his head. "You conned us into the bet Major. Admit it."

"I did nothing of the sort," Peabody answered. "I bet I could hold the onion and potato bags out before me, in one hand, for five minutes. I had no idea you would think I intended to hold the bags and their contents. Those onions and potatoes must weigh almost thirty pounds. I can't help it if you all misunderstood the terms of the wager."

Doc Carmichael poured a cup of coffee and told us all to resign ourselves to the plain and simple facts of the matter. We had been victimized. "Beware the wounded tiger," he told us. "Last night we wounded Peabody's wallet. I should have known he would exact his vengeance. I should have known better than to bet with him this morning."

Lefty was still unhappy with his unexpected loss of fifty dollars. "At the very least, he could admit to some sense of shame from the way he suckered us into the bet," he muttered.

"No, Lefty," Carmichael answered. "I've know this reprobate for more time than I would admit in public. I've watched him engage in various scandalous and nefarious behaviors, but I can't remember a single instance of him ever showing even the slightest hint of an indication that he might have a conscience."

Peabody turned to the doctor. He dropped his jaw and widened his eyes in feigned surprise. "You slander me," he said to him. "Granted, I have seldom, if ever, strayed from a life of commendable virtue and have had little reason to experience shame." This time it was Doctor Carmichael who dropped his jaw and widened his eyes in real surprise. "But," the Major continued, completely disregarding the doctor's reaction, "if you'll give me a moment or two, I'm sure I'll be able to remember an instance – perhaps two – when I have been genuinely embarrassed."

Doc Carmichael said "Hah!"

"Want to bet?" asked Lefty. Then he thought better of it and added, "I didn't mean that literally, Major. It was just a matter of speech."

Peabody sat at the table and affected an attitude of concentration. Mr. Olsen opened the wood stove oven, put his hand inside and calculated the temperature to be hot enough to bake the breakfast biscuits. He put a tray of them in the oven and began to fry the potatoes. During all this time, Peabody appeared to be in deep thought. From time to time he slowly shook his head from side to side as he considered and then rejected occasions when he might have been ashamed. Finally he smiled and said: "Eureka! I have found one." He got the attention of everyone.

"It was in Uruguay. Last year. We flew to Montevideo and then to Mercedes where we got into a Suburban and drove to Estancia Ninette. That's a ranch owned by Hector Sarasola. Hector's land contains an infinite number of doves and a substantial population of pigeons, ducks and perdiz. I had only a passing interest in the dove, pigeon and duck. I went to

Uruguay to hunt perdiz.

"Perdiz, as the name suggests, is a member of the grouse family. It likes an open, grassy kind of habitat and when threatened, it prefers to run on the ground. It flies only as a last resort. A good dog is essential to the hunt. Fortunately, the Estancia Ninette also serves as home to a number of well-trained Brittany Spaniels. Hector's own dog must be the reincarnation of one of the world's legendary human bird hunters. I've never seen a dog so eager to hunt.

"The dog would find a perdiz, perhaps two, three or even four gun ranges from a hunter. It would hold a rigid point. Even though the bird ran, the dog would remain motionless until the hunters were close. Then it would break the point and follow the scent left by the running bird. I once watched that dog as it closed in on a bird. It crouched until its belly nearly touched the ground and it practically crawled the final feet before coming to an almost lying-down point.

"In four days of hunting, Hector's dog never bumped a bird. If a perdiz was hit, the dog always found it, regardless of how far it may have sailed. The animal had a soft mouth. Its enthusiasm for the hunt was patent. Tail movement, eye concentration, short breath panting - I swear, the dog smiled when it brought a bird back for hand release. A few words, maybe a pat on the head and the dog raced back to the field to find another perdiz. He worked so hard and so well, some of the hunters actually apologized to it when they missed a shot.

"On the last afternoon of the hunt, I was on my way back to the truck, ready to call it a day. The dog, however, had a different idea. I was walking along a fence line on the upper part of a large field thinking great thoughts about perdiz hunting at Estancia Ninette. I lost track of the dog. When I turned I saw him, nearly an eighth of a mile behind me, frozen on point.

"I don't know how long he had held that point, patiently waiting for me to come to him, but it must have been for some time. When I got to him, he broke his point and began to follow the scent of the bird that had plenty of time to scurry away in the grass. The dog followed the running bird for a goodly distance, then pointed and waited for me. When I arrived, the bird had, again, moved away. The dog broke point and repeated the process. On the fourth point, the bird flushed well within gun range. I've never seen a dog work that well.

"You can imagine my feelings when I fired and missed." Major Peabody lowered his eyes, obviously moved by the telling of the story.

Lefty broke the silence. "I can understand your embarrassment," he said. "It must have been acute. The last shot of the last day of the hunt. The dog worked so hard and then you missed. You let the dog down and didn't have another day to hunt over it and make amends. What must that dog have thought of you?"

The Major looked up. "Oh, I didn't give a damn about what the dog might have thought." he said. "I was hunting with Hector. I was ashamed because I knew he was going to tell everyone about it."

Homo Homoni Lupus

Major Peabody was not his usual ebullient self. He left part of his rack of lamb untouched and even waved off a second after-dinner drink. When Major Peabody refuses a quality Fundador brandy from Spain's Jerez de la Frontera, it is obvious all is not right in the world. We left the restaurant and drove back to the Major's apartment in silence. After an evening at Bookbinder's, it is Peabody's usual custom to ask me to join him for a libation in his quarters. On that evening, no such invitation was extended.

I parked the car, accompanied him into his building and, uninvited, entered into his apartment. Wordlessly, he sat in his favorite wing back chair and seemed to stare off into empty space. Silence and contemplation are not Peabody characteristics. This was, indeed, strange behavior. I could not leave him in such a somber and morose mood. I decided it was incumbent upon me to raise his spirits. When I returned from the kitchen and handed him his drink, I asked if he was feeling well.

"I'm perfectly all right, thank you," he answered. "I've been thinking." He paused for a few seconds and then added: "That's all, merely thinking."

"About what," I casually asked and, at the same time, sunk into one of his overstuffed chairs, leaving no doubt that I intended to stay until my curiosity was satisfied. Peabody sipped from his Scotch and water and then looked up at me. I had purposely mixed it on the potent side. He set the highball on the end table. "Oh," he answered, "I was thinking about the various failures of mankind and how so many of Mother Nature's experiments have gone wrong."

"Come now, Major. It isn't that bad," I answered, hoping to engage him in conversation and get him to forget what was really bothering him – whatever that was.

"It isn't?" he asked. He seemed surprised. "Of course it is," he said, answering his own question. "Homo sapiens is racing toward extinction at a faster pace than that of some of the old gal's other disasters. The Hairy Mammoth, the Pterodactyl and the Great Auk come to mind." I looked quizzical. "Don't look so quizzical," he ordered. "In spite of what some of your tree hugging friends contend, extinction is not necessarily a terrible thing. I applaud it. Extinction is not all that bad.

"Think about it," he continued. "I enjoy walking in the autumn woods in search of the Ruffed Grouse. That enjoyment would be substantially diminished if I had to be on the lookout for prowling Saber-toothed Tigers. I'm glad they are extinct."

"I don't think anyone would be in favor of saving a predatory animal like the Saber-toothed Tiger," I said.

"You don't?" He asked and again seemed sincerely surprised. "There are organized groups of people who have successfully hindered the advancement of their own economy by demanding protection for such extinction bound species as blind minnows living in underground caves. Your friends proclaim the coming extinction of the caribou - animals they claim are so stupid they can't find their way around, over or under an oil pipe. They insist our government spend considerable amounts of taxpayers' funds to protect various bugs whose importance in the earth's life cycles is, at best, insignificant and irrelevant. What makes you think they won't decide to clone the Saber-Toothed Tiger?

"The population of the United States takes every

50

opportunity to nourish, sustain and protect vicious and destructive animals that represent a danger to our continued survival as a species. At every opportunity, it insists upon re-electing them to Congress. If the Homo sapiens had any sense of self preservation, all politicians would have already gone the way of the Saber-toothed Tiger."

"You're over-reacting," I objected. "I see no danger of the extinction of the human race. Oh, perhaps in a billion years or so, the universe may implode into a single black hole and do us all in, but even the possibility of that happening is infinitesimal. Certainly it isn't anything that should cause us to worry until a few more eons have passed."

Peabody sipped his drink. Without looking at me he said: "We'll all be gone long before everything is sucked into that black hole. Apparently you don't believe in evolution. If Darwin is right, and I suspect he is, only the fittest will survive. The human being is not the fittest. We don't stand a chance in the survival business."

"Of course, I believe in evolution, Major. What's that got to do with it?"

"This planet, my young friend, is a giant laboratory and we are nothing more than the latest in a series of experiments. Ages ago Mother Nature tried the "Too Big To Fail" theory and created the dinosaurs. When that experiment turned out to be a bust, she went to the opposite extreme and gave tiny creatures a go at it. The cockroaches and ants have stayed the course and mosquitoes have hung around, too, but, by and large, Mother Nature wasn't satisfied with them and continued with her tinkering.

"She embarked on her latest experiment. She selected a middle sized, timorous creature - our own distant ancestor - and gave it opposable thumbs. Nevertheless, it should be obvious to every one that she gave us only limited intelligence.

Brain power was not one of her primary considerations." Peabody sighed and returned to his Scotch and water.

My work was cut out for me. I had seldom seen Major Peabody in such a dejected and somber mood. I promised myself I would bring him out of it before I left his apartment.

"But Major Peabody," I said "Look how far we have advanced since the days of that distant ancestor. We've defeated all the threats that have faced us - smallpox, the black plague, cholera, yellow fever. We've harnessed fire and the atom, too. We've extended our life expectancy from mere years to decades and some people now live for more than a century. These aren't the characteristics of a species on the verge of extinction. These are unmistakable signs of progress."

"Progress? Progress?" Peabody snorted. "All we have done is to eliminate some of the microbes and viruses that can cause our demise. That accomplishment, I might point out, has exacerbated the world's terrible overpopulation problem. Sickness and disease are not the major problems facing mankind. In the final analysis, they have nothing to do with our extinction. Mankind doesn't need their assistance. We'll kill ourselves off without any help from them." He concluded his argument with three words: "Homo homoni lupus".

"And just what does that mean," I inquired.

"It translates from the Latin as 'man is a wolf to man'. It is an entirely accurate assessment of the condition of the Homo sapiens. Our own past attempts to commit species suicide have all failed only because we have been technologically incompetent. Within the next few hundred years we will correct that oversight and develop the ability to kill every member of our own race. We won't hesitate for a moment. Down deep, each man hates his fellows."

"That's pure nonsense, Major," I objected. "We humans give millions - no - billions of dollars to universities, to the

Salvation Army and to a myriad of other charities. You overlook the work of the churches, the food kitchens and the Shriner's hospitals. The impulse to help one's neighbor is far more widespread than any of mankind's meaner motivations."

Peabody set his drink down. From his expression I could see he was giving serious consideration to my argument. I believe he nearly nodded his head in agreement. He looked up and asked: "Do you really, really think so?"

"Of course I do, Major. Of course, I do.

* * * * *

Man is, indeed, a wolf to man. The predator had caught me. What else could I do when Major Peabody calmly asked: "Then I suppose you will provide me with three hundred dollars to tide me over until the first of the month?"

Woodcock - 2

"I'll come back on the Friday morning flight, my boy," Major Peabody informed me as the departure of his flight was announced. "It is my hope as well as my expectation that this will be a most productive hunt." Exuding optimism, he picked up his carry-on and walked toward the station where he would present his boarding pass. He smiled at me and added: "If the dogs are behaving well and if the birds are flying and if my shooting eye and reflexes have maintained themselves, upon my return, we'll celebrate with a modest get together at my apartment on Saturday. It will feature hors d'oeuvres of regal quality."

Just before he walked down the tunnel to the airplane the Major said he hoped the lovely Stephanie and I would be able to attend. Then he told me he had already invited her. He paused for a second or two and, with what I am sure was supposed to look like an afterthought, he added: "When we've finished with the hors d'oeuvres, we can all go out to dinner. Does Bookbinder's sound alright?" Before I could respond, he turned and disappeared down the ramp.

Peabody's invitations to join him for dinner whenever he returns from one of his hunting forays are one of his standard operating procedures. Such invitations presume I will cover the costs of the dinners. This causes me no concern. I always expect it. His mention of Stephanie and Bookbinders was merely a gentle reminder that I should be financially prepared. It was his statement about the hors d'oeuvres that both startled and worried me.

The Major was on his way to Maine. One of his hunting companions told him the Woodcock migration was underway and the birds were pouring down from Canada. The Major considers the Canadian Woodcock to be illegal immigrants. He dedicates a portion of every autumn to discouraging them from entering the country without proper documentation. He and his 20 ga. Lefever planned to again try to stop them near the border.

The little I know about Woodcock comes from conversations with Major Peabody. In the more elegant restaurants in France, he claims, it is not unusual for the entire bird to be cooked – including the feathers and the insides. What is more, he also tells me it is not unusual for French types to eat the product of such cookery – insides and all. I suspect they don't eat the feathers, but I may be wrong. Peabody assures me there are people who like the heavily liverish taste of Woodcock and think it is a delicacy. The Major is not one of them.

He once told me the best recipe for the preparation of Woodcock consisted of soaking them for twenty-four hours in a marinade composed of equal parts of garlic, kerosene and rabbit droppings. That marinade, he further explained, will remove only a small part of the bird's objectionable flavor. This makes it necessary to take an additional step. To protect the environment, the marinated bird should then be buried deeply underground in granite or by using the same methods employed for the disposing of primary atomic waste.

The Woodcock is the one bird Major Peabody will hunt, but will not eat. I've never tasted one and I don't intend to taste one. If Major Peabody won't eat them, I won't eat them. Now are you beginning to see the reason for my worry? If Peabody couldn't afford dinners at Bookbinders, could he afford hors d'oeuvres of regal quality catered to his apartment? Clearly, that question has to be answered in the negative. That meant he was planning to prepare the canapés. I worried that he was going to prepare Woodcock appetizers.

The thought of the Major bringing Woodcock from Maine and forcing me to eat them made no sense at all. Did he want to punish me for some transgression I may have inadvertently committed? No, he suggested I bring the lovely Stephanie with me. Peabody likes the lovely Stephanie. He'd do nothing to injure her. Certainly, he wouldn't feed her Woodcock appetizers.

Peabody had something else in mind. He was planning some outrage, but I hadn't a clue of what it might be. I spent two sleepless nights wondering what he had in mind. I spent two more days wondering how I might avoid whatever trap he was setting for me.

I couldn't simply call in sick. Peabody's invitation to the lovely Stephanie made it impossible for me to decline. The lovely Stephanie would accept no explanation or excuse if I failed to escort her to the affair. I considered all other alternatives, including suicide. In desperation, I clung to the hope that Woodcock were not on the Major's soiree menu, or that the birds would eschew their autumnal migration and stay in Canada, or that the weather would be so bad the Major couldn't leave the cabin and engage in the hunt.

They were all forlorn hopes.

Peabody returned to Philadelphia on Friday morning. He smiled and waived at me as soon as he entered the terminal. He was carrying a brown corrugated box about as big as three or four good sized dictionaries and almost completely covered with duct tape. It was not a good sign. "I couldn't trust them to the baggage compartment," he said as I pessimistically studied the parcel. "Don't worry, young man," he continued, "They're packed in dry ice are should be in a pure and uncorrupted condition."

"Woodcock," I ventured, hoping for the best.

"Yes, Woodcock" he answered, "Fresh from the forested lowlands of northern Maine."

When I heard his answer, for the first time in my life I fully understood the meaning of the term 'sinking feeling'. When I finished carrying the Major's baggage and shotgun into his apartment, the last words I heard from him were: "Don't forget. You and Stephanie. Tomorrow afternoon." I had little more than twenty four hours to save myself from the horror of eating Woodcock and from the horror of losing the affection of the lovely Stephanie.

* * * * *

Major Peabody answered the knock on his door. "Ah, Stephanie," he exclaimed, "you look radiant – radiant and wonderful." Then he turned to me. "And you young man," he paused, surprised. "You look terrible. Good Heavens man, whatever happened to you?"

"I've had shome very bad luck," I answered through clenched teeth. "My jawsh musht remain immobile for at leasht shix daysh. After driving you home yeshterday, I shlipped in the bathroom and fell againsht the shink. I fracshured my jaw. I had to have it shecurely wired shut."

Things were going fairly well for me. The lovely Stephanie was filled with sympathy and concern. Phrases like: "Oh, you poor dear" and "Can I do anything for you" fell from her sweet lips. She even offered to change the bandage on my jaw. Of course, I bravely declined. Had she done so, she would have easily seen through the charade. There was neither bruise nor fractured jaw because there had been no accidental fall. My jaws, however, were tightly wired together.

When he was young and a bit naïve, my dentist told me, he was inexperienced in recognizing the snares and pitfall of the world. He was talked into taking a bite of a baked Woodcock. The experience left deep scars upon his psyche. He agreed to aid and abet my plan to avoid eating Woodcock by installing the wiring that caused my cheeks to puff out. It also affected my speech and made it impossible for me to eat solids. He told me he would remove it all in a week. Six days of minor discomfort was a price I was willing to pay. I would be on a liquid diet and might lose a few unwanted pounds, but I wouldn't have to eat the Woodcock.

"What unfortunate timing," Peabody said as he led us into his dining room. "The Gourmet Gods must dislike you."

The Major's table was adorned with candles and covered with a lace table cloth. On it, chateau bottled red and white wines, wheat crackers, Brie and Camembert, whitefish caviar, a slab of smoked salmon and an entire smoked Pheasant were predominantly displayed. Had my jaw not been wired, it would have dropped. "Major, you old dear," said the lovely Stephanie and she gave him a peck on the cheek.

"One of Doc Carmichael's friends is an avoid smoker," Peabody explained. "I don't mean cigarettes or cigars," he said as he knocked an ash from his H. Upmann into a convenient tray. "I mean game," he said. "He loves to smoke wild game," and he waved toward the salmon and the pheasant laid out on the table. "He caters fancy weddings and the like. Can you believe it? He likes Woodcock. I traded him a dozen of the vile things for this spread."

Of course, I couldn't enjoy the dinner at Bookbinders either.

Gun Control

It was nearing the end of the month and I expected Major Nathaniel Peabody would be in his usual unacceptable financial condition. I was, therefore, surprised when he not only invited me to a dinner at Bookbinder's, but volunteered to pay for the dinner. It wasn't the only surprise I received that evening.

Throughout the meal, the Major's eyes as well as the conversation sparkled. We were enjoying a Spanish brandy and he was in process of lighting an H. Upmann cigar when our pleasures were interrupted. A man approached our table and addressed Peabody with a hearty, cordial, but patently insincere greeting. Then, uninvited, he sat at our table and our pleasant conversation was put on hold.

We both knew the man. We had often seen him on a local evening television news program. He read the canned news reports that were placed before him. He did his very best to sound like David Brinkley and look astute. He failed to achieve either goal. On Saturday mornings, he hosted a program devoted to local Philadelphia events. He impressed neither of us.

After watching those Saturday morning programs, any one with an analytic ability better than that of a garden slug would immediately conclude the man would never die of conservatism. He supported anything that could be labeled "liberal", no matter how insane. That support was as automatic and predictably as the movement of a compass needle seeking out magnetic north.

It was understandable. In the television news commentary business, being liberal is a condition precedent for promotion from a rural to an urban and, finally, to a national television news position. Conservative newscasters have a high hurdle to jump. Anyone seeking advancement had better be liberal.

Peabody was quite aware of the newsman's bias. The television station's sportscaster had interviewed the Major on the occasion of the opening of the duck hunting season. After the segment had been taped, Peabody watched as, off camera, the newscaster chastised the sportscaster for favorably publicizing what he referred to as a "horrible blood sport designed to drive all waterfowl into extinction".

Now, at our table in Bookbinders, the newsman gave no hint of his animosity toward hunting. "People are interested in you, Peabody," he said. "The station got quite a bit of mail after your interview with our Sports Department."

"Oh?" was the Major's cautious response.

"Yes," the newscaster continued, "quite a bit of mail. The viewing public's interest in a personality like you is a newsworthy event and news is my business." Major Peabody wondered if the man's business was coloring the news or reporting it. However, he just smiled and, with difficulty, kept his mouth closed.

"The station has scheduled a program to investigate the societal effects of the development of hunting," the newscaster announced, smiling his phony TV smile. "It will be taped on Saturday afternoon and it would be a privilege to have your participation. We do want the input of a hunter with your reputation. Will you join the panel?"

The Major accepted the newscaster's invitation. His acceptance of the invitation was my second great surprise of the evening.

When the newsman left the table, I expressed that surprise. "Surely you know he has a long record of open antagonism to guns and hunting," I said. "Surely you must be aware of what you're letting yourself in for. Surely you know he'll do everything possible to show the societal effects of the development of hunting are similar to the societal effects of atomic warfare."

"Of course," Peabody answered. "I know his record, but I couldn't refuse him. He put me in an untenable position. If I didn't accept, he'd claim I was frightened. During his show I'd be the empty chair he and his friends would point to. If I didn't accept his invitation, no one would be there to defend hunting and gun ownership."

* * * * *

On Saturday afternoon, I drove Peabody to the television station. When we arrived at the studio, the crew, the host and his other guest were waiting for us. The Major was quickly ushered to the set where the taping would occur. Brief instructions were given, someone counted backwards from five and the host introduced the program.

"Good morning, ladies and gentlemen of our viewing audience," he began. "The steep rise of gun crime in both urban and rural America is one of the most serious problems facing our nation. At an alarming rate, mothers and innocent children are being maimed and killed in drive-by shootings and during the numberless other senseless crimes involving firearms. This morning we will investigate ways to eliminate gun crime and return to a more civilized society."

I noticed one of the television cameras was constantly trained on the Major. If he ever burped, scratched his nose or showed an unattractive reaction, that portion of the tape was sure to appear when the telecast aired. Peabody, however, showed no outward reaction to the sandbagging.

The host's introduction of the other panelist, an anti-gun activist, was lengthy and embarrassingly favorable to him. Peabody wasn't treated that gently. With a subtle touch of contempt in his voice, the host described the Major in three short sentences.

"Nathaniel Peabody is here to try to defend gun owners. Peabody has developed a reputation with people who hunt. He is reported to have killed more of our birds than any man in the State."

The next fifteen minutes were disgraceful. Peabody wasn't given any opportunity to engage in the discussion. The host threw softball questions at the activist who quoted questionable statistics and painted frightful pictures of atrocities involving the use of weapons. In response to the question of how to reduce gun crime, the activist presented his plan. It consisted of five elements.

First, the importation for all firearms into the United States would be outlawed.

Second, the federal government would be given the exclusive right to manufacture firearms.

Third, the federal government would be given the exclusive right to sell and distribute firearms.

Fourth, all weapons currently owned by anyone other than military or the law enforcement personnel would be registered.

Fifth, a federal agency would be created for the purpose of collecting all registered weapons and storing them in government armories to be built at various strategic locations within each of the fifty States.

In deference to the hunting fraternity, the gun control activist was willing to allow a modification to his draconian measures. People planning a hunting venture could get their guns from the armories by filing a written application at least seven days in advance and by passing a background check. If there were no disqualifying results, a government employee would deliver the hunter's weapon on the condition that it be returned to the armory within 24 hours.

The TV newsman, after nodding affirmatively during the gun controller's explanations, agreed that the plan would certainly eliminate all gun crime and lead to world peace. Then he turned to the Major and asked: "That looks like a reasonable plan, Peabody. What do you think?" The Major's response was immediate.

"I am deeply moved by my colleague's passionate report of guns slaughtering infants as they lay helpless in their tiny cribs," he said. "The spread of gun crime in the United States is a cancer deserving more than mere serious attention. It deserves action. I am pleased to announce my own interest in supporting my colleague's five point plan."

The Major's statement was more than merely an unexpected surprise. It was a shock. The gun control activist's face clearly showed the extent of his astonishment. The startled TV newscaster straightened up, knocked over his coffee and dropped his pencil. Standing off-camera, I couldn't believe my ears. I'm sure all three of us shared the same thought. Major Nathaniel Peabody had gone mad.

Peabody disregarded our reactions and repeated his approval of the program. "I'm pleased to offer my support for your admirable plan to save humanity from the outrage of gun crime," he said. "If gun owners and gun controllers can agree to work together to accomplish common goals, no force in this grand Republic can defeat us. Together, our two groups can eliminate not only one but another equally serious scourge of mankind."

Peabody looked directly at the gun controller and said: "I

believe gun owners will support your program to eliminate gun crime if gun control enthusiasts will, in turn, support the hunters' five point program designed to eliminate venereal diseases from the face of the earth."

While both opponents were still wordless, the Major described the five elements of the hunter's venereal disease control program.

"First, all gun control people shall be registered and fitted with male and/or female chastity belts.

"Second, the keys to the devices will be deposited in a vault located in the same government armories where hunter's firearms have been deposited.

"Third, those of the gun control persuasion who want to commit sex must fill out an application, giving seven days prior notice.

"Fourth, both parties to the application must go to the appropriate armory for blood tests and background checks.

"Fifth, if the tests and background checks show no disqualifying result, a government employee will meet with them at the home, motel or Chevrolet back seat identified in the application. He will unlock the devices, wait for half an hour, re-lock them and return the keys to the armory vault.

"If both of the programs my colleague and I espouse are adopted, we can all be assured the hunters' program for eliminating venereal diseases will be just as effective as the gun controller's program for eliminating gun crime."

The taped program never appeared on television screens.

Misdirection

It was a beautiful autumn day. As the chlorophyll drained from the trees, the leaves showed their various yellow, orange and rusty red colors. There was a hint of crispness in the air. Pessimists would interpret it as a warning of what would come in January and February. I suspected Major Peabody would be hunting somewhere. Nevertheless, I telephoned him and was half surprised to find him at home. I invited him to a drive through the countryside. I was sure he'd enjoy it.

During this particular drive, however, the Major seemed vaguely pre-occupied. He stared out of the automobile window and initiated little conversation. He wasn't in the mood for small talk. I wondered why. I respected his wish for privacy, but the reason for his introspection attracted my curiosity. The 'why' of it became obvious when, in the late afternoon, we returned to the Major's apartment.

Peabody didn't bother hanging up our outer clothing. He dropped our coats on a convenient chair and I immediately attended to my usual assignment - the task of preparing a libation. I noticed the only Scotch under the sink in Peabody's kitchen was an almost completely depleted bottle of The Macallan. The absence of a back-up supply of aged, single malt Scotch whisky was an unmistakable signal that Major Nathaniel Peabody was again devoid of funds.

I guessed it was the Major's miserable financial condition that explained his unaccustomed silence as well as the reason why he wasn't hunting. The accuracy of my guess was further confirmed minutes later. When I brought his drink, Peabody was reaching for a cigar. I noticed there was only one H. Upmann left in the humidor. No Scotch and no cigars? Undoubtedly, Major Peabody was flat broke.

The Major is a proud man and would never admit he was in a desperate financial circumstance. I sincerely wanted to help him, but I didn't know how to do it. If he were to ask for an early delivery of his monthly Spendthrift Trust remittance, I would have to disappoint him, just as I have had to disappoint him so many times in the past. The terms of the Trust are clear. He has to wait until the first of the month. That meant Peabody had to wait four more days before getting his check.

I've known the Major for some years and during that time I have never heard him ask for a loan. If he ever borrowed, he knew he probably wouldn't pay it back. Peabody would not stand for being called a welsher. I presume this is why borrowing is strictly against his principles. He wouldn't accept an offer of even a short-term, non-interest bearing loan.

If I attempted to give him a few hundred, he would call it "charity" (unless, of course, he 'earned' it through some thoroughly unscrupulous deception). Accepting charity would be an admission that he had become dependant on others. Such an admission was an anathema to Major Peabody. Moreover, he would despise me. By making such an offer I would be telling him I considered him incapable of managing his own affairs. I believe he must have had at least a vague suspicion that it was the truth, but he would never admit it.

With those avenues to immediate financial assistance closed, the Major's only alternative was to resort to chicanery. Peabody has often (too often) maneuvered me into a card game or some ridiculous wager that consistently ended in a reduction in the width of my wallet. I'm tired of delivering his monthly remittance to some hunting camp in some distant and terrifying place inhabited by bears, snakes, unshaven men and other wild animals, only to be greeted with the words: "Major, your patsy has arrived."

Many, many times I have promised myself I would never again be taken in by Major Peabody's crafty maneuverings. This time I was forewarned. I knew he was broke and I suspected he would be planning some outrage designed to separate me from my money. No, I didn't want to be bamboozled, but, I will admit it, I did want to help him out.

Associating with Major Peabody is an educational experience. You learn misdirection and duplicity. You learn how to allow a person to mislead himself. I took a page from the Major's book. I put my mind to it and found a way to help him without him knowing it. The Major won't accept money, but he would accept cigars and Scotch whisky. I acted before he could spring whatever trap he had envisaged.

"The Macallan," I said appearing to savor the highball. "I thought you preferred The Glenlivet."

"I did," he answered. "I did until I found out the company was owned by Frenchmen. I'll be damned if I'll buy any of their products."

"Well, that's lucky."

"What's lucky?"

"You preferring The Macallan," I answered. "There's a sale on the stuff. If I had known, I would have laid in a supply. I don't think it's too late. I'll be back in a minute. I picked up my coat, drove to the nearest liquor store and bought a case of the Macallan. I wish it had been on sale. I also wish the Tobacco Shop had a sale on the H. Upmann 48x6 ring Corona Brava cigars. After the tobacconist quoted the best price he could offer for a box of twenty five (a hundred and fifty dollars) I must have turned pale. He asked me to sit down and brought me a glass of water.

* * * * *

I set the case of Scotch on the floor and placed the box of cigars on top of it. Peabody took my coat, started for the closet and then changed his mind. He dropped the coat on a chair and opened the case of The Macallan. He handed me a bottle and suggested I prepare a drink, saying: "We should taste it to make sure some scoundrel hasn't mislabeled it."

I performed the duty. When he took a sip and informed me it was, in fact, legitimate, I suggested we celebrate the cigar and Scotch sale by having dinner together.

During dinner, I brilliantly performed another coup. "Oh, Major," I said, squinting my eyes and slowly shaking my head. "I completely forgot. The lovely Stephanie wanted to know if you would be free for dinner tomorrow. Please don't say no. I'll be in serious trouble if you can't make it and she finds out we've had dinner tonight without her."

I was in a good mood as I drove home after delivering the Major to his apartment. It was worth the investment. I had provided him with food, with drink and with cigars. He never suspected I had slipped one past him.

* * * * *

Major Peabody opened his hallway closet door. He hung up his coat and then kicked his hunting boots to the side. After sliding the attorney-purchased case of the Macallan into the place vacated by his hunting boots, Peabody reviewed the supplies stored on the top shelf of the closet. Four additional bottles of the Macallan and two unopened boxes of Dominican Republic cigars rested there.

Peabody returned into his living room. He sat in his

favorite wing back chair and put the twenty five H. Upmann cigars in the humidor. It had been a successful day.

"Let's see," he mused. "Dinner with the counselor and the lovely Stephanie tomorrow and dinner with Doc Carmichael on Monday. We'll talk about a November duck hunt on the Chesapeake and he'll pick up the tab. I'll have to figure out something for Tuesday. Yes," he said, "this worked out much better than I planned. I would have settled for the dinner at Bookbinders, but I managed to get a case of The Macallan and a box of cigars, too."

The Three Little Pigs

The lovely Stephanie called at four-thirty. Without notice of any kind, her five year old niece had been left with her. The child was going to spend the night and the lovely Stephanie was unable to find a baby sitter on such short notice. She told me our plans for dinner and an evening at the Philharmonic would have to be cancelled unless I could find someone to watch over little Clara. After a number of unsuccessful attempts to locate someone willing to spend Saturday night with the little girl, things looked grim. Then I remembered Major Nathaniel Peabody.

The Major always claimed he liked dogs and little children. That he liked dogs - hunting dogs in particular - was beyond question. As far as I was concerned, the jury was still out on his alleged attraction to little children, but I was desperate and willing to try anything. I called him and was pleasantly surprised when he not only professed great competence in the baby sitting business, but added that he would be overjoyed to tend the lovely Stephanie's niece.

Peabody finished the conversation by stated he would not accept a penny more than fifty dollars for his services - "payable in advance" was the way he put it. Perhaps I shouldn't have told him I was so desperate. Nevertheless, I happily agreed. Pleased by my good luck, I drove Peabody to the lovely Stephanie's Bryn Mawr condo. The fates continued to smile upon me. We left for dinner before any personality conflict erupted between the Major and little Clara.

Frankly, I expected to be confronted by a screaming child and a disheveled Major when we returned to the condo after midnight. However, excepting only the discovery that a prized antique tea cup had been used for a cigar ash try, all was in good order. An empty bottle on the tea table attested to the fact that Peabody had found the lovely Stephanie's supply of Spanish Sherry. He was dozing in an over-stuffed chair and little Clara was peacefully sleeping in the guest bedroom. No furniture had been broken and there were no other signs of a fight.

When I drove him back to his apartment, Peabody told me Clara was no problem at all. He told her a bedtime story and she went to sleep without any fuss.

* * * * *

"Now, Clara, honey," Major Peabody softly said, "Take a little sip of this. Now, snuggle up in your bed and Uncle Nathaniel will tell you the story of the Three Little Pigs."

"Oh, Uncle Nathaniel, I already know the story and the big bad wolf scares me."

"Well now, honey, people tell lots of lies about wolves. They've been given a bad rap. It's time you learned the truth. The false, shameless and disgraceful stories that have vilified the wolves for so many years should be exposed. You know Uncle Nathaniel wouldn't fib to you, don't you?"

Little Clara looked dubious, but she didn't say anything.

"Wolves, Clara, honey," the Major continued, "are not wanton killers. You shouldn't be afraid of them. Now, just settle back and Uncle Nathaniel will tell you the true story about the three little pigs. Here, take another little sip of this."

"Once upon a time, during the Great Depression of the 1930s, the only food many families had to eat was the fish and game they poached from the forests, lakes and streams. The animals fared no better than the humans. At times, they, too, went hungry.

"The wolves ate better than most of the four footed animals because they were accomplished hunters. Pigs, being some of the most intelligent members of the animal family, also ate well and survived those Depression years without any great inconveniences.

"Actually, the pigs did better than the wolves. The 1930s were known as 'hard times', but that's when the phrase 'fat as a pig' came into being. It is still in general use today. In those days nobody every said 'fat as a wolf'. Nobody uses that phrase today. Wolves didn't and don't eat as well as pigs. Wolves are nice guys, just like human hunters - especially bird hunters - nice guys.

"Like I said, pigs are smarter than wolves. If they caught Freddie the Woodchuck and ate him, they wouldn't brag about it and tell everyone how delicious he was. Pigs knew their success in finding food would make other hungry animals envious, so they kept their mouths shut.

"Take another little sip, honey.

"Because wolves are good hunters, they liked to publicly brag about their hunting ability and, Clara honey, I'm afraid, they liked to exaggerate - just like today's bird hunters. Moreover, outside of their immediate families, wolves wouldn't share their food with other animals. What with their bragging and their refusal to share food, wolves became quite unpopular with the other animals that often went hungry.

"Nevertheless, it was a murder trial involving three pigs that gave the wolves their bad reputation. It all began in the mid-1930s when a wolf disappeared and a report was filed with the Department of Missing Wolves. The sheriff, a bulldog named Sam, investigated the report. He went to the missing wolf's den. It was in Disarray. Disarray is in a rural Township in the western part of the County. It should not be confused with the State of Disarray which is in Washington, D. C. The den was in shambles. Lamps were broken and personal papers were scattered about. The unmistakable signs of a struggle were everywhere.

"Sheriff Sam called for assistance from the State Crime Lab. It sent its Hoof Print expert to the scene and he found three different sets of cloven hoof prints entering the wolves' den. Armed with that information, Sheriff Sam interviewed a number of local white tailed deer, thinking some of them may have killed the missing wolf to avenge the wolves' depredations of their herds. The deer had air-tight alibis. At the time of the wolf's disappearance, they were all at the State capitol, marching in support of a bill that would outlaw deer hunting.

"Continuing with the cloven hoof clue, the sheriff was able to separate the sheep from the goats, question the flocks and eliminate all of them from complicity in the crime. Then he directed his attentions to the pig community. He began his inquiries by searching the homes of three porkers, brothers and notorious law breakers.

"Here honey, have another sip of this.

"In the pigs' back yard, Sam found a wolf skin, stretched and drying in the sun. This aroused his suspicion. Inside the building, he found a stew pot bubbling on the wood stove. Mixed in with onions, truffles and carrots, he found bones that might have been those of a large dog or, perhaps, those of the missing wolf!

"Sheriff Sam accused the three pigs of killing the missing wolf and arrested them on the spot. The District Attorney brought charges and the stage was set for a jury trial in the matter of State -v- Three Little Pigs. The pigs hired a weasel with the reputation of being one of the cleverest criminal attorneys in the county and a plea of Not Guilty was entered.

"It was generally believed the DA had an air-tight case. The bones and the hide were the corpus delicti and the stew provided the motive for the killing. Moreover, DNA taken from the pigs, when compared with the DNA of the pig bristles found in the wolf's den, placed the pigs at the scene of the crime. However, in retrospect, observers note major errors in the preparation of the State's case.

"First, the presiding judge who heard the case was an old hoot owl, not known for having developed an appreciable degree of wisdom. He had been elected to the bench because of the overwhelming support of his fellow lawyers. It is universally recognized that attorneys favor only those candidates for judicial office who are dumber than they are. They don't want smart judges. They want ones they can fool. Perhaps the DA should have asked for a different judge.

"The DA made no attempt to counteract the weasel attorney's influence in the matter of jury selection. The weasel convinced Judge Owl that the constitutional right to a 'trial by a jury of your peers' in this case meant all jurors had to be pigs.

"Finally, the DA's presentation of his case was decidedly ragged. He spent so much time describing the intricacies of DNA testing that half the jurors became confused rather than knowledgeable. The other half went to sleep. After someone awakened Judge Owl, he had to wake up the jury. When the DA rested his case, the weasel went to work.

"The first witness attacked the character of the deceased wolf. He claimed he was an experienced shepherd and an expert of wolves. He testified wolves were outlaws who deserved no protection from the legal system. If a wolf had been murdered, he contended, the act should be classified as 'praiseworthy homicide" and the murderer set free.

"In his cross examination, the DA failed to show the shepherd's anti-wolf bias. He didn't even tell the jury the witness was known as 'the boy who cried wolf'. Then the weasel dismissed the DNA evidence by claiming the letters meant 'Damn Near Anybody'. The all-pig jury could be seen nodding in agreement.

"In a surprise move, the weasel, called the defendants to testify. The first pig testified that the wolf attacked him, chased him into his house of straw, huffed and puffed and blew his house down. Terrified, the first little pig ran to his brother's home for sanctuary.

"The second little pig corroborated the testimony of his brother and tearfully told the jury how the wolf, snarling with bared teeth, circled his house of sticks trying to find a means of entrance. Finding none, he huffed and puffed and blew the house down, leaving only a pile of rubble and an unpaid mortgage. He and his brother narrowly escaped the ravening wolf and managed to get to the home of the third brother.

"The third little pig then took the stand. The fearsome wolf, he claimed, was unable to destroy his house of brick, but entered it by sliding down the chimney. In fear for their lives, the three little pigs then hit the wolf over the head with iron skillets, killing it on the spot. There wasn't a dry eye in the jury when he finished testifying.

"Judge Owl, remembering how the wolf had bragged about catching and eating his aunt Maude, gave the jury instructions clearly biased in favor of the three little pigs. The jury deliberated for less than an hour before returning a verdict of "Not Guilty.'

"And so, little Clara, to this day it is the common, but completely false belief that the villain of the story was the good natured wolf and the good guys were those three lying pigs. Now you know the truth."

Rara Avis

Major Nathaniel Peabody rattled the ice cubes in his empty glass. I took it from his hand and, when restored to its original condition, returned it. He sipped and nodded his approval. On the following morning he and three of his friends would leave for South Dakota where they would celebrate the opening day of the pheasant hunting season. Pheasants were definitely on the Major's mind.

He talked about them throughout the evening meal at Bookbinders. He talked about them when we drove back to his apartment. Now, seated in his favorite wing back chair, enjoying libations and a cigar, he continued to talk about them. During the entire experience, I limited myself to polite comment. ("Is that right, Major?", "How interesting, Major", "Really, Major?", and "You don't say, Major?")

Frankly, Major Peabody told me much more about pheasants than I cared to know - much, much more than I cared to know. A change of subject was long overdue. "Very interesting, Major Peabody. Very, very interesting," I said and, hoping to sidetrack him, added: "Do you know such interesting things about other birds? Cardinals? Or Rose Breasted Gross Beaks?"

"You've just gone up in my estimation, my boy," he replied. "I didn't realize you, too, were fascinated by birds. I thought you were only pretending to be interested in pheasants. You've opened the door to a whole new series of topics." (Inwardly, I shuddered.) Peabody leaned back in his chair and

I prepared myself for a long evening.

"You are probably acquainted with the Kiwi," he began. (I thought it was a fruit.) "It is an exceptionally strange bird." (Well, at least he wasn't going to talk about pheasants.) "It's the only bird that has its nostrils at the end of its beak. Isn't that curious? The female Kiwi is the size of a chicken but it lays an egg as big as an Ostrich egg. That's astonishing."

"Amazing," I said and tried, unsuccessfully, to think about something else.

"I agree completely," Peabody said. "It is a wonderful bird. It is nocturnal and it spends most of the daylight hours in a nest burrowed underground. It can't fly. It doesn't have any wings. It is an irritable and bad tempered fellow and it isn't easily domesticated. Unlike its distant cousin, the Rarie bird, the Kiwi is not a good pet."

"The Rarie bird?" I questioned.

"Yes, the Rarie. Have you ever seen one?" he asked. I never heard of a Rarie bird, let alone see one, but I had no opportunity to admit it. Major Peabody didn't wait for an answer to his question. He steamed ahead at full speed. "I'd be surprised if you had. Few people know about them and fewer have ever seen one. The Rarie is a Western Hemisphere apteryx. Usually a shy and retiring wingless bird, the Rarie is found only in a few wild and uninhabited areas in the Sierra Madre Occidental Mountains in the Mexican State of Durango.

"I've been unable to find any in-depth studies of the bird. Some commentators say the Rarie is a species heading for extinction. Others say the population remains stable, but the bird's territory is limited because of its as yet undetermined, but probably narrow, climatic or environmental life requirements. Certainly the Rarie is not common and I would not hazard a guess as to its future. Though they are not game birds, I have come to admire them. The Rarie is a pleasant and sociable thing. I know this to be a fact from personal experience.

"Years ago, I visited the estancia of Francisco Lopez. For well over a hundred years the Lopez family has operated a cattle ranch in the State of Durango. The Lopez ranch is large, containing tree groves, scrub land, planted grains, waterways, mesquite and cacti. It has all the elements needed to attract large flocks of White Winged Doves. That explains why I always accept don Francisco's hunting invitations with shameless speed.

"I recall my first trip to the Lopez ranch. In those days I knew nothing about the Rarie. You can imagine my surprise when I first saw one. Unlike the New Zealand Kiwi, the Rarie is not nocturnal and prefers to peck around for seeds during daylight hours. At don Francisco's request, one of his vaqueros captured one and brought it to the hacienda.

"The Durango Rarie is much smaller than the Kiwi. It is about the size of a tennis ball and is covered with narrow, pinnate, iridescent plumage - like short bits of individual peacock feathers. The bird has large blue eyes and relatively short legs. It isn't aggressive and, apparently, easily bonds with human beings. I was immediately attracted to it. Of course, I wanted to bring it back to Arizona, but there was a problem. The United States Department of Agriculture specifically prohibits the importation of Rarie birds.

"I can understand why the Department doesn't want to run the risk of bringing a new species into the country. Since the first Brown Tree Snakes were inadvertently introduced into Guam, the island has been overrun by them. It is estimated there are 1,300 of them per square mile. You can imagine their destructive effect on that island's ecosystem in general and, in particular, the local bird populations. In the United States, various State Natural Resource Departments have their hands full in combating other alien imports such as the Zebra Mussel, Eurasian water milfoil and that disagreeable looking, air breathing, land crawling, voracious predator, the Asian walking fish.

"The U S Department of Agriculture had no idea of the extent or character of the impact the Rarie might have on our environment, but they have had many disagreeable experiences with the unintended consequences occasioned by importing foreign species into the country. I applaud them for their caution. Nevertheless," Peabody admitted, "I wanted a pet Rarie.

"At that time I was stationed near Flagstaff, almost a thousand miles from the Rarie's home territory in Durango. Raries can't fly and even if motivated by the most powerful of mating season urges, I doubted any of them would walk from Durango to Flagstaff. Though my knowledge of biology is fairly limited, I believed the bird would not be able to reproduce all by itself. Therefore, I came to the conclusion that one pet Rarie would cause no serious environmental damage to northern Arizona.

"It was a difficult decision, but I decided to make a single exception to my rule of never violating a government edict." (I don't believe the Major saw my automatic expression of surprise when he suggested he was reluctant to violate rules, governmental or otherwise.) Peabody looked down and sheepishly admitted: "I smuggled a mature male Rarie bird past the Nogales Customs Station and into my off-base quarters in Flagstaff.

"I was right," he continued. "The Rarie didn't upset local ecological patterns. However, the opposite was true. The northern Arizona environment had a powerful effect on my Rarie. It began to grow at an alarming rate. It doubled its size every week. At the end of two months, it was 500 times its original size. Three weeks later, when it was 4000 times the size of a tennis ball, something had to be done.

"At three in the morning of a moonless night and with some difficulty, I loaded the Rarie onto my neighbor's snowmobile trailer. Under cover of darkness and undiscovered by local law enforcement personnel, I drove out of town. The sun was rising when I arrived at the south rim of the Grand Canyon. I disconnected the trailer and pushed it to the edge of the rock walls that dropped straight down to the Colorado River, far, far below.

"I untied the bird and quickly lifted the tongue of the trailer. The Rarie began to slip over the back edge. It tried to hang on but couldn't. I was sincerely attached to that bird. A tear appeared in my eye when the bird's grip on the tilted trailer began to loosen. Then, falling into the abyss, it cried out: "It's a long way to tip a Rarie."

Educating Bruce Golightly

"My name is Bruce Golightly. I belong to various organizations dedicated to supporting World Peace, protecting the environment, preserving the culture of stone-age savage cannibals living in the Amazon jungles and fighting injustice whenever any of those organizations tells me it occurs. I am particularly proud to be President of the Philadelphia Area Society To Protect Our Deer, Our Wooded Lands, The Whales And Our Environment Generally.

"Last month, one of our members, a lovely lady named Stephanie, brought an escort to one of the Society's meetings. She presented him to me. He was an attorney. I don't remember his name. Three days later, I happened to find the man dining with someone at Bookbinders. Stephanie's friend invited me to join them and introduced his companion, Major Nathaniel Peabody, a retired army officer.

"I didn't think I could ever become friendly with an army person. Some of them, I am told, swear. I know they shoot rifles and sometimes drop bombs on poor foreign people, but Major Peabody proved to be an exception. By the end of the evening, I was calling him 'Nathaniel'. He didn't seem to mind when I refused to call him 'Major'. I consider all army and navy officers' titles to be particularly objectionable. By using them we condone violence.

"It was inspiring to find a man who, despite his ugly, anti-social military background, was, in fact, a true environmentalist. During our conversation, I discovered Nathaniel loved animals - dogs in particular. He told me he spends hours and hours giving them exercise in the woods and fields. The lawyer reacted to Nathaniel's admission by snorting.

"I must tell you, my opinion of Stephanie's attorney friend plummeted as my opinion of Nathaniel soared. With thinly disguised raised eyebrows and occasional not quite muffled laughter, the lawyer seemed to denigrate all of Nathaniel's statements displaying his sincere interest in protecting our feathered and furry friends.

"Nathaniel confided that he and some of his associates were engaged in a humanitarian project to collect Ruffed Grouse, Hungarian Partridge and those beautiful Chinese Pheasants. They intend to take the birds to a taxidermist and have the more perfect specimens mounted. Those mounts will be presented to orphanage school in order to give those unfortunate children a glimpse of wild life. The attorney actually spit out a mouthful of food, when Nathaniel explained his praiseworthy project. Imagine!

"Nathaniel whispered into the man's ear. I'm sure he politely asked him to behave. Soon thereafter, the lawyer smiled and excused himself, leaving me alone with Nathaniel. When he found I had spent all of my life in urban surroundings, Nathaniel was amazed. He showed equal surprise when I admitted that very few of the members of the Society To Protect Our Deer, Our Wooded Lands, The Whales And Our Environment Generally had never been in the woods.

"You can imagine my delight when Nathaniel invited me to join him and two others for a week-end in an Upper Michigan study group retreat. Of course, I quickly accepted the kind offer. Nathaniel had left his wallet in his apartment and after I insisted in covering the bill, we parted - newly made friends.

"On Friday we flew to Michigan and rented an automobile. You may not believe this, but sometimes we drove for a mile or even more through unbroken forest lands without seeing a single house or telephone pole. It was scary. As we left the graveled road and turned onto a two rutted trail, some of the trees were less than six feet from me. I was delighted to see so many of them. I wanted to stop the vehicle, get out and hug them, but it was getting late and the sun was going down.

"We arrived at a rude cabin long after dinner time. Nathaniel introduced me to his two friends. When I asked them if they were going to help collect the Bonasa Umbellus Umbellus, they looked first at me and then at Nathaniel in a most peculiar way. One of them said something in what I took to be the Chippewa language. He said: 'Wotinell zeetawkin bowt.' I don't know what it means.

"At this point Nathaniel noticed the evening meal's dishes had not been washed. He took me to the sink, brought hot water from an old-fashioned kettle that had been sitting on the top of a wood burning kitchen stove and assigned the task to me. Then he engaged his friends in quiet conversation. I suppose he was telling them I was a kindred environmentalist spirit. In any event, after the dishes were washed, dried and stacked, the somewhat chilly reception I had received was replaced by warm inquiries into my well-being and careful attention to my comfort.

"One of the men brought out a glass gallon container of what appeared to be dark reddish cider vinegar, but they were playing a joke. It wasn't vinegar at all. Nathaniel told me the man had carefully poured three liters of quality chateau bottled French Burgundy into the glass jug. I didn't catch the name of the chateau. I believe they referred to it a 'Day Go Red'. It was tasty. In accordance with local custom, the after dinner cocktail hour lasted for three hours.

"One of the men took a chunk of wood from the box beside the pot bellied stove. 'This is beech,' he told me. 'Notice the smoothness and color of the bark. Then he showed me the butt end of the wood. 'You can tell if the season was a dry or a wet one by looking at the thickness of any year's growth,' he informed me.

"I was greatly impressed by his intimate knowledge of the environment. I listened attentively while all three talked about such strange trees as hemlock and tamarack and yellow birch - ones you'd never see in our yards in the Philadelphia suburbs.

"One of Nathaniel's friends went outside and returned with a huge, heavy thing - a piece of iron, flat on one end and sharpened on the other. It was affixed to a long wooden handle. When I asked what it was, Nathaniel told me it was called a 'splitting maul'. I learned it is used to break larger chunks of wood into pieces that would fit into the wood stoves. I was fascinated. I thanked Nathaniel when he promised to show me how to use it.

"By this time I had taken quite a few glasses of the Day Go Red. Nathaniel's friends had insisted my glass be re-filled whenever it became half empty. I went to the sleeping room and took off my shoes. I was exhausted by the fresh air and excitement. I laid down on the bottom bunk and almost immediately fell into a deep sleep that lasted until the morning.

"After I washed, dried and stacked the breakfast dishes, true to his word, Nathaniel took me outside to a very large pile of blocks of wood. He set one piece on its end and told me to aim about one-third of the way between the edge of the chunk and its center. He said I should use the same sort of swing golfers use when they slice their ball into the rough and then bang the heads of their drivers into the ground. Nathaniel said splitting wood would improve my golf game. One of the men quoted Kaiser Wilhelm II - 'Split your own wood and it will warm you twice.' Sage advice, indeed.

"Nathaniel and his friend embarked on their Ruffed Grouse

collection expedition, leaving me with the splitting maul and the pile of wood. If I say so, myself, I became quite adept at splitting wood. By late afternoon when my friends returned to the cabin, I had split the entire pile. That evening after I finished the dinner dishes, we enjoyed some more of the Chateau Day Go. It must be some kind of sedative. I again slept through the night, almost fully dressed.

"The next morning, one of Nathaniel's friends taught me how to make wood piles. While the three men went into the forests in search of specimens of the Bonasa Umbellus Umbellus, I was allowed to pile all of the wood I had split during the previous day.

"On Monday morning, we returned to Philadelphia and Nathaniel and I parted company. What an instructional week-end it had been. I am indeed lucky to have Nathaniel and his two ecologically sensitive associates as mentors and friends. At our next annual meeting, I intend to nominate all three to share the Society's Annual Gentleman or Gentlewoman, As The Case May Be, Guardian of the Environment Award."

Oh, the Humanity of It All

Major Peabody lit a cigar, blew a smoke ring, smiled and tried to convince me he had a consuming interest in the welfare of youngsters. His interest was such, he informed me, that he had already invited two of his friends to join him and volunteer for a humanitarian endeavor aimed at insuring adequate supplies of milk for the tiny tots. When I registered mild disbelief, he came forward with a more complete explanation.

In Iowa, pheasants were destroying local corn crops. Corn, the Major informed me, formed a part of the diet of cows which, he further informed me, produced milk. "When I discovered that cow's milk was the same stuff small children drink," he told me, "my better nature came to the fore. What could be more altruistic than eliminating the nasty pheasants that destroy the corn crops used to feed the cows that produced the milk that nourished the tiny babes?

"I immediately looked for men who shared my altruistic sentiments and, of course, I thought of you. My plan," the Major told me, "is to get such a group together, travel to Iowa and do our very best to reduce the population of the marauding, ravenous pheasants. It will be our purpose to save the corn crop thereby providing adequate sustenance to the local dairy herds and, thus, protect little children from the terrible effects of a milk shortage."

Translated into plain English, the Major wanted me to go to Iowa with him. His hidden agenda was quite obvious to me. I knew he wanted to engineer some kind of bet which I could never win and/or draw me into a poker game. This time I would escape his trap. I was in the middle of drafting a very intricate Estate Plan for James Larson, one of Philadelphia's most successful and clever Personal Injury attorneys. I was quite pleased when the man complimented me after he reviewed a rough draft of the Trust, but I do wish he hadn't used the phrase "tax evasion".

I had a good excuse to decline the Major's invitation. That trust document and the allied incorporation, the drafting of deeds and the arranging of stock transfers all required a good deal of time and attention. In addition, I had no inclination to go to Iowa and had no interest in contributing to the Major's financial well-being.

On more than one occasion Mr. Larson had mentioned his avid interest in shotgunning. I suggested the Major invite him in my stead. And so it came to pass.

* * * * *

The hunters arrived at their destination in the late afternoon. They ate, enjoyed a libation and had time for a friendly poker game. The following morning, the sun had risen and the hunters, still in their motel room, were dressing and preparing for their imminent humanitarian campaign. At that moment, however, Peabody's thoughts were directed at neither the hunt nor the welfare of the children.

His attentions were directed toward one of his companions. Major Peabody carefully considered the civil damage trial attorney, James Larson. When the poker game began on the previous night, Peabody recalled how Larson had asked: "I can never remember - does a straight beat a flush or does a flush beat a straight?"

At the time, Peabody thanked the Poker Gods for

delivering the attorney into his hands. The fellow's subsequent performance at the card table, however, was not something calculated to fill Peabody's gizzard with unbounded joy. Larson carefully conned the Major into investing far too much in second best hands. The Major and his friends had been injured by the man's display of poker expertise.

Major Peabody scolded himself. "I should have known better," he complained. "How could I have failed to recognize him as a con artist? This man is a successful Personal Injury lawyer. He has been schooled in guile, trickery and deception. He has been trained to convince juries of make-believe injuries. He has made a business of misleading knowledgeable judges. As far as I know, he has been able to avoid being charged with perpetrating crimes against humanity, but the man is nothing more than a devious knave. I admire him so very much."

After breakfasting in the restaurant adjacent to the motel, the Major engineered an opportunity to speak privately with the attorney. He complimented him on the subtle ways he mislead them at the poker table and the cunning mechanisms he employed to convince losers that their hands deserved one and sometimes two additional pointless bets. Then the Major got down to brass tacks.

"With a little more training and experience," Peabody informed him, "my hunting companions might become mediocre marksmen. Correct me if I am wrong, Larson, but I suspect you are a damned good shot?" It was a question, not a statement. The lawyer looked at Peabody and cautiously nodded. He suspected the Major was trying to entrap him.

"I will admit," the Major continued, "that I have the reputation of being able to hit what I shoot at." He paused for a bit before adding, "I believe it might be profitable for us to join forces."

The attorney could recognize a kindred spirit when he saw one. The scheme was hatched on the spot. On the first day, Larson agreed to fire with a complete disregard for the range of his shotgun. He further agreed to miss on nearly every occasion. Peabody agreed to have an "off day", but not shoot so badly as to raise suspicions on the part of his usual hunting compadres.

When the first day of the hunt had ended, the attorney had not a single pheasant in his game pouch. Peabody had tried to shoot poorly but, nevertheless, had killed three birds. Later in the evening, when the single malt Scotch and the cigars had been distributed, the Major made his move. Peabody suggested a contest. It would begin on the next morning. He and Larson would spot each of the others a one bird advantage and, at the end of the remaining three days of the hunt, the team with the most birds would split the pot.

Before Peabody could propose the size of the wager, both of his friends declined to participate. They were gun shy. They knew the Major well enough to avoid betting with him. Sad experiences taught them he had a way of winning nearly every bet he made. Peabody's expression telegraphed his disappointment. It clearly proclaimed, "Well, I tried."

The Personal Injury lawyer was conditioned to turning disaster into triumph and he seized the opportunity. He told the Major's friends that he expected they would want to recover their poker loses. Abandoning the Major's team effort proposal, he suggested that he and the other hunters create two pools. Each of them would put $500 into one of the two pots. Since he would be involved in both of the pots, he would contribute a thousand dollars, putting 500 into each of the two pots. Peabody wouldn't be involved in the bets. He'd have to sit this one out.

"If I can only win one of the pots, I'll break even," Larson said in an effort to strengthen the appearance of his inability to master the shooting of a bird in flight. Peabody's friends took the bet.

Later, Peabody again had a private conference with the lawyer. "I was afraid they might react that way," the Major told him. "I was afraid they'd turn down my proposition, but, they accepted yours. I'll put up 500 dollars to cover my end of the bet."

Then Larson disappointed Peabody by refusing to take his money or recognize his value in setting up the scheme. "Sorry, Major. You're out of the picture," he told him. "I made the deal with them. I put up the thousand dollars. I'm the one doing the shooting and I'll reap all of the rewards."

On the following day, a startling metamorphosis took place. Larson was heard to exclaim such things as: "Good heavens! What a lucky shot," and "I never expected to hit it," and "Is that my bird? Didn't either of you shoot?" Unexpectedly, the same metamorphosis affected the other two hunters. They were heard to say: "Great Scott. I was falling down went I pulled the trigger," and "I shot at the first one and the second one dropped."

At noon, the men were having a field lunch of sandwiches and coffee. Each of Peabody's friends was well ahead of the lawyer. The Personal Injury attorney arose from his camp stool and stretched. He looked at his fellow hunters. Both were trying, unsuccessfully, to look innocent.

"This charade has gone far enough," he announced. He pulled out his wallet and shuffled through the wad of bills stuffed into it. He handed $250 to each of the other hunters and then gave $500 to the Major, saying, "I presume each of your friends was going to split the pot with you." The Major nodded and the other hunters smiled.

"It's my own fault," Larson said. "I should have suspected

something. I believe you and these two thieves have been hunting together for some time?" It was a question and the Major nodded an affirmative. "Your snare was well hidden and your confederates were very convincing," the attorney admitted. "It was a well engineered deception."

He was silent for a moment while he considered how he had been conned. Then he looked at the Major and asked: "Did you, by chance, ever practice personal injury law?"

Quack, Quack, Quack

Major Nathaniel Peabody is not a cold weather person. About the time of the Winter solstice, I see the beginnings of a decidedly negative change in his attitude. It displays itself first in late December with a "bah humbugging" of the yuletide season. In January, it intensifies. Complaints of the gray skies, soot covered snow and slush punctuate his conversations. In February, the Major shows signs of melancholic depression. He begins to stray from reality in early March. His eyes film over and he begins to speak, wistfully, of dogs and shotguns.

Doctor Carmichael has diagnosed this malady. He claims a peculiar strain of DNA found in some men make them susceptible to what he quaintly refers to as "Cabin Fever". The drug companies have been unable to find an antidote for the sickness, but, fortunately, the disease and all of its symptoms disappear soon after the advent of the vernal equinox.

From January through March, whenever I deliver the Major's first of the month Spendthrift Trust remittances, I spend as little time with him as possible. Being with him for any period of time during the first quarter of the year is a dreary experience unless he has been able to temporarily avoid the contagion by embarking on a shotgunning expedition to some warmer climate.

Last Winter was one in which the Major was confined to his Philadelphia apartment without any seasonal interruption. He invited me to dine with him and, in spite of my knowledge of his usual wintertime wretched attitude, I accepted. Someone,

I thought, had to lift him from what I was sure was his then current mood of dark dejection. I destroyed my budget by investing in a bottle of 25 year old Macallan single malt Scotch and bravely made my way to his living quarters.

I hung my overcoat and hat in his closet, turned and saw the lovely Stephanie approaching me. She gave me a very brief kiss on the check and said "Happy Birthday." Yes, it was my birthday, but I had no suspicion the Major would plan a surprise party. He seated me next to the fireplace in his own favorite wing backed chair and treated me as if I were a lord.

The lovely Stephanie brought me a goblet of Chardonnay and the Major, showing not the least sign of melancholia, kept it filled. For just a moment, I had the suspicion the Major had some hidden agenda behind all this kind treatment. I quickly dismissed the thought as being unworthy of me.

The dinner was excellent. Peabody browned chopped onions, garlic and pieces of Ruffed Grouse dredged in flour. He added mushrooms, basil, thyme and parsley and skillet cooked them in white wine and lemon juice. Wild rice and asparagus spears covered with Béarnaise sauce completed the entrée. A brace of Pedro Domecq Fundador brandies followed and I was, indeed, quite mellow when we retired to the living room.

The lovely Stephanie disappeared into the kitchen only to immediately re-appear with a candle decorated cake inscribed with the message "Happy Birthday, Darling". The lovely Stephanie is not given to expressions of infatuation and the inscription on the cake convince me I was making progress with her. I made a wish and blew out the candles. No, I won't disclose the wish I made.

I opened the presents. The lovely Stephanie gave me a five year membership in the Greater Philadelphia Area Bird Watcher's Society. She is on the Board of Directors and actively participates in its projects. She heads the Society's as yet unsuccessful attempt to get the State legislature to enact a law requiring all cats to be fitted with tiny electronic devices that sounds a loud alarm whenever the animal comes within ten feet of a bird.

Though she considers the killing of any kind of bird to be a tragedy of huge proportion, the lovely Stephanie likes Major Peabody. She finds him charming. Though she may suspect the truth, she has convinced herself Peabody enjoys walking in the woods and fields. She doesn't mind him taking a dog with him, but would be happier if he didn't carry a shotgun. When he is in her presence, the Major is careful to avoid any talk of hunting. He does nothing to abuse the delusion that he is merely enjoying healthy out-of-doors exercise.

The Major gave me a box of 25 H. Upmann cigars, a duck call and a tape designed for instruction in its use. The gift of the cigars didn't surprise me. I don't smoke. Peabody knew he'd get the entire benefit of that present.

I was alarmed by the gift of the duck call. I suspected it was meant to give the impression I liked to kill ducks. It looked to me like Peabody was trying to destroy any possibility of my developing relationship with the lovely Stephanie. I decided to immediately mount my defense. "Whatever might this be?" I questioned, hoping to convince the lovely Stephanie that I was not a duck hunter.

"It's a duck call, silly," she responded. "The Major and I thought you should have one."

I was thunderstruck. The lovely Stephanie and the Major thought I should have a duck call? Was she serious? Was she underwriting the hunting of ducks? Had Peabody somehow convinced her it was alright for me to become a duck hunter? Peabody saw my confusion and provided an explanation for her curious behavior.

He explained duck calls were tools that should be carried and used by all serious bird watchers. As soon as I became expert in its use, he said, members of the Greater Philadelphia Bird Watcher's Society, including the lovely Stephanie, and I could visit lakes and wetlands where I could call in ducks and others could count them, take pictures and ooh and ahh as, in beautiful formation, they gracefully sailed over our heads.

The lovely Stephanie's enthusiasm was almost unlimited. "Major Peabody makes such marvelous suggestions," she purred, smiling at him. I tumbled to what Peabody must have had up his sleeve. The dear old fellow had become a match-maker. He cleverly arranged a way to give me opportunities to be close to the object of my affection. Perhaps the lovely Stephanie and I could plan weekend trips to distant marshes.

Thus motivated, I eagerly dedicated myself to the business of becoming an expert in the art of duck calling. It was not an easy task. After a full day at the office, I'd return to my apartment and spend a few hours listening to the tapes and blowing on the duck call. There was some unpleasantness when neighbors called the police. I was forced to cease and desist or face the consequences of a citation for Disturbing the Peace.

Major Peabody came to my rescue. He allowed me to practice in his apartment and hinted that an occasional bottle of single malt Scotch might be an appropriate recognition of his assistance. The Major's neighbors had become accustomed to strange noises coming from his apartment. At various times in the past, they lodged complaints against him, but his abilities to fend off the authorities, together with the subtle revenges he was able to exact, conditioned them to grin and bear it - or, at least, to bear it.

During practice sessions with Peabody and Doctor Carmichael, I soon realized my duck calling was much better than the doctor's. In reality, the doctor's calling did nothing more than frighten ducks away. Over the ensuing summer months, I became an even more expert in the art and you can imagine my satisfaction when the Major told me I was ready to move from practice session to real tests in the field.

Peabody and Doctor Carmichael allowed me to accompany them on their opening day duck hunting expedition. I sat between them in their blind and proved my ability to convince ducks to come into gun range. Since then, I've traveled with them to many sloughs and waterway, honing my ability to attract ducks and bring them in for closer observation. Peabody tells me that by next spring, given continued field experience, I will be ready to call ducks for the members of the Greater Philadelphia Bird Watcher's Society. I am sure the lovely Stephanie will be impressed.

A Philosophic Interlude

Major Nathaniel Peabody and I dined at Bookbinders and, as had become our usual custom, we returned to his apartment for an after-dinner libation. I paid for the dinner. That had also become one of our usual customs. We sat in his living room and the Major began the conversation.

"When Prudhomme wrote 'Power corrupts. Absolute power corrupts absolutely,' I suspect he hit the bull's eye," Major Peabody said. He lifted the cover from the humidor that contained what was left of the 25 H. Upmann cigars he had given me when we celebrated my birthday. He took one of them and returned the humidor to the drawer in the end table next to his wing back chair. The cigars had been in his humidor ever since my birthday party. He knows I don't smoke.

As soon as the Major quoted the Prudhomme aphorism, I knew he was up to something and I suspected it had to do with money. It was the 22nd day of the month. A few days earlier, he had returned from a five day Hungarian Partridge hunt in South Dakota. It was nearly a certainty than he had managed to spend the rest of his money and was in his usual end-of-month penniless condition. He was not entitled to another Spendthrift Trust remittance until nine days had passed.

It is intriguing to watch Major Peabody spin his web in an attempt to trap me into financing him during the last days of those months when he is destitute. Those webs often entrap me. I contribute dinners, cigars and single malt scotch on an all too regular basis. His moves to secure early trust fund distributions are clever, even ingenious. I've learned some of the signs that predict the advent of his too often successful frauds.

The reference to Prudhomme was not made for the purpose of any kind of philosophic discussion. No, Peabody was up to something and the warning flags were flying. He was about to launch an attack on the assets of the Peabody Spendthrift Trust or, worse, on mine. I prepared myself to refuse to extend any requested form of financing and made a mental note to be extremely cautious in all conversation with him. I limited myself to a non-committal "mmmmmm" and an innocuous "Perhaps you are right".

"I am convinced," Peabody continued, "that people's distrust of our own government is directly proportional to the power it assumes. The country's reaction to Congressional attempts to destroy the Constitutional right of gun ownership comes to mind. I consider the people's fear and their distrust of their government are entirely admirable reactions, founded in solid common sense and worthy of encouragement."

Personally, I've come close to firearms only when delivering the Major's checks to some hunting camp and on the one occasion when he insisted I buy an expensive shotgun and accompany him on a Cuban duck hunting trip. I bought the weapon. It has received precious little use. I'm afraid of it and won't have it in my lodgings. Like the 25 cigars he gave me as a birthday present, the gun is stored in the Major's apartment.

That Cuba trip is not one of my favorite memories. We returned to Philadelphia via Canada. The Canadian Customs Inspector found the Cuban cigars Peabody tried to smuggle into the country by shoving them down the barrels of my shotgun. I had to pay a hefty fine.

As any sane person knows, any legislation passed by Congress for the purpose of controlling firearms would be just as successful in stopping crime as the 18th Amendment was successful in stopping drinking. The Major, however, was developing a thesis for some purpose aimed directly at my wallet. It would be prudent to change the subject, so I interrupted him.

"Didn't Prudhomme also write: Comparisons are odious?" I asked.

"Why, yes he did, my boy," was the Major's mildly surprised response. Peabody always showed mild surprise when anyone under 60 years of age indicated he had read something other than newspapers, trade journals, best sellers or the comics. Peabody lit the cigar and continued.

"While I accept the validity of that first Prudhomme adage, I'm not convinced the one you quote is equally accurate. If we were to compare my ability to understand the sneaky terms you lawyers use when drafting Spendthrift Trusts with your ability to understand them, doubtlessly I would find the comparison odious. You, on the other hand, doubtlessly, would find the comparison to be pleasant." Inwardly, I smiled.

"But," the Major added, "if we were to compare my ability to use a shotgun with yours, I would find the comparison delightful and you would find it odious. Your Prudhomme quote is, at best, only half right."

I remembered our Cuban hunting experience. Peabody was correct. I found paying the fine was odious. Peabody found my discomfort to be pleasantly humorous.

Peabody blew a smoke ring and watched it rise and slowly dissipate before adding: "Prudhomme has another maxim I usually find to be of questionable accuracy. I refer to the one that proclaims: Property is theft. It is favored by the liberals who love to quote it in defense of what they call 'income re-distribution'.

"Earning the money to buy property requires a lot of time.

Once purchase money is earned, there are additional costs involved in property ownership. There are real estate taxes, insurance premiums, property improvement costs and a myriad of other expenses involved in owning something. Even something as basic as owning a dog involves expenditures for flea powder, collars, dog food and veterinarian expenses.

"Taking all allied expenditures into consideration, property is not theft. It is a representation of a lot of time spent working to get the money to buy it and take care of it. My initial reaction is: Prudhomme was wrong. Property is not theft. Property is a lot of work."

The Major thought for a second and then said: "On the other hand, perhaps Prudhomme had something else in mind. Among the reasons Walt Whitman gave to explain why he thought he could turn and live with animals was the fact that they were not infected with the mania for owning things.

"If a man owns neither lawn mower nor home, he need not paint the house or mow the lawn. With no color TV, he need not spend his Sundays watching football when he could be hunting pheasants or ducks. I can see how property can be considered as a thief - a thief of a man's time that can never be recovered. What do you think?" he asked as he leaned back in his wing back chair and blew another smoke ring.

During Major Peabody's time in the service, he led a nomadic existence. He was never in one place long enough to buy a home. Now his assets consisted of the furnishings of his apartment, a few shotguns and his clothing. They were all he needed and all he wanted. I began to understand why Major Nathaniel Peabody had so few worldly goods. To him, ownership represented an unwanted cost and an unwanted responsibility.

I thought of my associates at Smythe, Hauser, Engals & Tauchen - their homes, their horses, their automobiles, their golf clubs and their wives. They were slaves to them. They were tied down by them. Their labors at the office were required in order to keep and maintain their various properties. Property seemed to control their lives. I compared them to the Major and concluded Prudhomme was right. Comparisons can be odious. In this comparison, the odium did not reach Major Nathaniel Peabody's side of the equation.

I also concluded property was theft. "Yes, Major, I believe you are right. Too many people fill their lives with things. Then they must assume the responsibility of maintaining them for the rest of their lives. Yes, property robs its owner of time."

Peabody rose from his chair. "For a younger man," he said, "you have a praiseworthy grasp on an important concept. Oh, the mania for owning things. It can destroy your life."

Later, it was time for me to go. As I put on my coat, Peabody took a paper from his pocket. He pressed it into my hand and said: "Since your unsuccessful attempt to smuggle cigars from Cuba, you have never used that Citori 12 gauge double. For you it is one of those properties that must be stored and cared for. It could lead to the destruction of your future happiness. Luckily, I recognized that danger.

"Yesterday I retrieved that burdensome bit of property from my closet and took steps to protect you from the perils of ownership. Here is the pawn ticket. I recommend you don't reclaim it."

Another Bear Story

It was the afternoon of the last day of the month. The Major was hunting grouse. During the previous afternoon, I had arrived at the cabin where he and his friends were staying. At the stroke of midnight, I'd give Peabody his check and immediately drive my rented car back to quasi-civilization. That same afternoon my flight would take me back to Philadelphia and the safety of my own apartment.

I suppose my troubles began when the Major talked me into going with him on what he described as a walk in the beautiful autumn woods. It would, he told me, be better than spending so much time all alone in an isolated cabin, far from medical attention. I immediately saw the logic of his argument, and quickly (perhaps too quickly) accepted his invitation.

We walked on a narrow trail that soon disappeared. I feared the possibility that I might be separated from Peabody, become lost in the woods and find myself alone with the rattlesnakes and bears and other ravenous beasts. That fear increased when I could no longer see the cabin. It took another jump when I could no longer see the smoke from the cabin chimney.

Finally I could stand it no longer. The fear of being alone in the cabin with no one to help if I became injured or ill was more than counterbalanced by the fear of encountering a bear in the woods. I went back to the cabin.

* * * * *

Major Peabody returned from his morning hunt, leaned his 20 ga. Lefever against the building and entered the cabin. I was standing there, waiting for him. As Peabody often reminds me, I had a water glass in my hand. It was only half filled with whisky. My eyebrows, he recalls, were located halfway to my hairline and my eyes were rounded in terror. I was ghostly pale and, occasionally, demonstrated what is meant by the phrase "involuntary shudder".

"What's up, young man," Peabody inquired. "You insisted on returning to the cabin. I gave you clear directions on how to get back here. I hope you didn't get lost. Calm down. What happened to you? You look like you've just seen a bear."

The presence of vampires, Frankenstein's monster, a wolf man or even a United States House of Representatives Democrat does not frighten me nearly as much as an encounter with a bear. I remember setting the water glass (now three-quarters empty) on the table and responding to Peabody's question.

"I left you at the creek bottom and went up the ridge," I said, "just like you told me. It takes a bend to the west and the sun hits its north side, just as you told me. I had no trouble finding that great big patch of blackberries. I started to walk around its edge to get to the top of the hill from where you told me I would be able to see smoke from the cabin.

"I must have stepped on that black bear. It jumped up right in front of me. Six inches in front of me. It was at least twelve feet tall. Big, blood stained fangs. Ugly face. Mean look about him. Bad breath, too. It let out a terrible roar. As soon as it roared at me, I bravely screamed back, turned and ran as fast as I could. Soon thereafter, I found myself back here in the cabin. I don't remember exactly how I got here. It was a close thing, Major."

(As the Major's attorney was talking with him, the black

bear - more than a mile away - was talking with one of its friends. "I was minding my own business," the bear said. "I was eating blackberries when I must have stepped on this guy. He jumped up right in front of me. He couldn't have been more than six inches from me. He was at least twelve feet tall. Big, blood stained teeth. Ugly face. Mean look about him. Bad breath, too. He let out a terrible scream. As soon as he screamed at me, I bravely roared back, turned and ran as fast as I could. Soon thereafter, I found myself here with you. I don't remember exactly how I got here. It was a close thing, Yogi.")

Back in the cabin, Peabody tried to calm me. "Calm down, young man," he said. "It was only a bear."

"ONLY A BEAR? ONLY A BEAR? Bears are vicious beasts. They think people are good to eat. They turn over peoples' cars and eat them. I mean the people, not the cars. They hate people."

"I'll admit they sometimes get hungry," Peabody said in soothing tones, "but they don't hate people. Some of them are downright friendly. Some of them go out of their way to help people."

I don't recall exactly what I said, but I think it was "Amazing," or something like that.

Peabody took the now empty glass from my hand and set it on the cabin table. "No, it's the truth," he said. "I know it's the truth because I have witnessed it." The Major added another substantial amount of Scotch to my water glass and poured out a dollop for himself. "Come," he said. "Sit and let me tell you about it." The Major eased himself into the frayed overstuffed chair next to the fieldstone fire place, lit a cigar and told his story.

"About thirty years ago, I was a Military Attaché at the U S Embassy in Manila. I made the acquaintance of a man named Li Chan. For most of Li Chan's life, he lived on Mondo, an island south of Manila. He was Chinese, but considered himself to be a Mondoan. Most people mispronounce that word. They put the accent on the 'do' and say moan- DOH - ann. Actually, the accent is on the last syllable. The word is pronounced moan-doh-ANN. To aid in that proper pronunciation, in the Philippines, the word is usually spelled Mondo-ANN"

I am now sure the Major's little digression was calculated to distract me from my then, so recent, terrible experience with that vicious black bear. I'll admit I became interested in the Major's story. He leaned back in the chair, sipped, puffed and continued.

"The island of Mondo is rich in native hardwoods. Li Chan was a lumber merchant. He owned and operated the only saw mill on the island. In those days, there weren't many roads. Li Chan had a fleet of tug boats. He used them to haul rafts of logs from island shoreline staging areas to his mill. He was well acquainted with the bays and inlets that were attractive to both local and migrating ducks. Most importantly, he was an avid duck hunter. That's how we got together."

"What's that got to do with bear?" I asked.

"Be patient. I'm getting to it. Terrible typhoons race through the Sulu Sea. From time to time, they devastate Mondo Island. Li Chan had to rebuild his mill every few years. He could afford to do it. There was big money in tropical hardwood, particularly teak. I was in the Philippines when one of those typhoons hit. Among other serious damages, it destroyed the Mondo Island Catholic Church. Li Chan ran the only real business there and, I'm afraid, he didn't pay his employees much more than subsistence wages. The Mondo-ANN natives were poor and the parish was just as poor. Rebuilding the church would be a problem for them."

"Bear, bear," I insisted. "You were going to tell me how

bear have so many nice qualities."

"I'm getting to it. I'm getting to it. I often managed to get to Mondo and hunt with Li Chan. When the ducks weren't flying, we'd sit in the blind and he would tell me about the local flora and fauna. Mondo Island abounds with interesting plants and animals but since you're in such a hurry, I won't tell you the fascinating facts about the Sulawesi Kus Kus. I'll skip directly to the Mondo-<u>ANN</u> Bear.

"Because of its gentle nature, the Mondo-<u>ANN</u> Bear has become extinct in most of the islands where once they were numerous. Many were trapped and taken to zoos where, unable to live in captivity, they soon perished. Today, the creature is found only on Mondo Island, a place where it faces no danger from zoo curators who are prohibited by law from landing on the island.

The Mondo-<u>ANN</u> Bear is large. Adult specimens weigh between four and five hundred pounds. In addition to their characteristically gentle nature, the animal can be identified be two unique features. It has opposable thumbs and it leaves a footprint that looks surprisingly like that of a small human being."

"Truly?" I asked.

"Truly," the Major answered.

"One morning Li Chan came to the Embassy. He asked for advice concerning a problem that developed on Mondo Island. Li Chan noticed his finished teak boards were disappearing from his saw mill. He also noticed finished teak boards were being used to rebuild the typhoon-destroyed Catholic Church. He suspected the priest was stealing lumber. Li Chan didn't want to become involved in a confrontation with the church, but finished tropical hardwood planks brought high prices on the open market. He didn't know what to do.

"Of course, I agreed to help my duck hunting companion. I

went to Mondo Island and climbed a tree. From high in its branches, I could watch Li Chan's lumber yard. If a thief stole any lumber, I intended to follow him to the church, catch him in the act and suggest he discontinue his stealing and avoid the publicity that would certainly be quite embarrassing to all concerned.

"The sun had begun to rise when I was roused from my dozing by the sound of boards being removed from a pile of lumber. By the time I crawled down from the tree and entered the lumber yard, the thief had left, but I could plainly see the small, fresh tracks heading straight for the church. I followed them and arrived at the church in time to see a Mondo-<u>ANN</u> Bear unloading the planks it had been carrying on his shoulder.

"It was obvious that neither the priest nor any of his parishioners were the malefactors. It was a gentle Mondo-<u>ANN</u> bear, coming to the assistance of a human being in need.

"The priest certainly appreciated the bear's help. I saw him place his hand on the bear's head and I heard him say: Blessings on thee, Mondo-<u>ANN</u>, Boy Foot Bear with Teak of Chan."

Carl Wussow's Spring Pond

It was October 20 and Major Peabody was going hunting. During the last half of that month, he usually went hunting for ducks and grouse. The terms of the Peabody Spendthrift Trust obligated me to personally deliver his first-day-of-the-month remittances. The Major expanded that responsibility to include driving him to and from the airport whenever he undertook a hunting trip.

I had already brought his suitcase to the van when he came out of his apartment building carrying a light brown pig skin Leg-o'-Mutton gun case containing his vintage 20 ga. double barreled Lefever shotgun. The weapon was his pride and his joy and he wouldn't let me touch it, let alone carry the gun case. He explained the reason with a terse statement. "You might, drop it."

Today, as he closed the outer door of the building, I noticed he carried only the pig skin case. From past experience, I knew he always took two weapons with him - the Lefever for the grouse and a 12 ga. for the duck. "Major," I called out to him. "You forgot your 12 ga. shotgun." Peabody paid no attention to my warning. He slid open the back door of the van and carefully placed the Leg-o'-Mutton on the seat. As he opened the door to join me in the front, I tried again. "Major," I repeated, but got no further.

"Let's go," he interrupted. "I don't want to miss the plane. I do like to be in the woods in mid autumn. It's a great time to be there. The greens of the spruce and balsam and the reds and yellows of the deciduous trees are a memorable sight." I couldn't believe Major Peabody would leave on his regular late October hunt without his duck gun. Now that he was sitting next to me, I decided to try again while we were still close enough to his apartment to easily return and get the missing gun.

"Major, I believe you've forgotten one of your shotguns," I said loudly, slowly and enunciating carefully, thinking he may be losing his hearing.

"No need to shout, my boy. I'm taking only my Lefever," he said, just as if that simple statement were an explanation. There had to be a method in his madness. Leaving his duck gun behind wasn't an oversight. My curiosity was killing me. We drove on in silence for a few minutes before he spoke again.

"I suppose your curiosity is killing you," he said. "There is a good reason for leaving the 12 ga. behind. I might as well explain it to you." Peabody leaned back, made himself comfortable, and told the story.

"Five or six years ago," he began, "I was invited to participate in a Ruffed Grouse hunt. The invitation was extended by a man I met during a previous South Dakota pheasant expedition. Frankly, I didn't particularly like the man. Normally I don't associate with a person who would ground swat a pheasant. Still, one must be willing to subordinate personal feelings if one is truly interested in securing opportunities to be asked to join upland bird hunts. I accepted the man's invitation.

"The other hunters were strangers to me. They were cut from the same cloth as my host. It was not a pleasant hunt. To name a few of the perpetrated outrages: shouts of 'I got him' rang out from men who hadn't fired a shot; a poker IOU wasn't honored; and, the only Scotch whisky in camp was blended. There was only one good consequence flowing from that entire misbegotten foray. My host had hired a local named Carl Wussow to serve as guide and camp cook.

"Carl and I got to know each other. During the first evening, we both apologized for being in the company of the others. Carl admitted he had a bad experience with the host. He told me he didn't get full payment for the food he bought for the previous year's hunt.   He had again asked to be reimbursement for those out-of-pocket expenses. He request was again denied.

"After preparing the next morning's breakfast, Carl quit. He left the camp and took his food supplies with him. I joined in the exodus and the two of us hunted together for the rest of the week. It was the beginning of a solid friendship. I now have a standing invitation to visit him and hunt on his land.

"Carl owns 160 acres in the Argonne National Forest. His quarter section harbors grouse, Woodcock, wild turkey (both distilled and two footed), deer and various other birds and animals. It also contains two pot holes and a spring pond. I've never been to the pot holes, but he took me to the pond.

"The substantial flow of water from a spring produces a waterway that curves like a scimitar. It's seventy or eighty feet across at its widest point and about a quarter mile long. Then it pinches together, gets some additional water from the pot holes and forms a stream which empties into the Brule River. The pond isn't very deep and I could easily see the gravelly bottom. Carl told me he caught trout there in the springtime before the sun and the weed growth raised the water temperature

"Of course, I thought about duck hunting. In answer to my questions, Carl eyed me speculatively and came to the conclusion I could be trusted. He took me to a knuckle of land that stuck out into the pond. A well camouflaged blind was concealed at its point. From the blind I could see both ends of the scimitar.

"Carl told me the pond wasn't always productive, but usually provided first class pass shooting. Both local and migrating duck seemed to have a natural flyway down the center of that scimitar. He told me I could use the blind. He also told me it was his secret place and warned me to keep my mouth shut.

"For the next three years, whenever I visited Carl during the duck season, I'd get up early. Carl would make a pot of coffee for me and then go back to sleep. I'd carry a dozen blocks to the pond, set them out and await the action. I've seen muskrats. I've seen otter. I've seen deer come to the pond to drink. I've seen eagles – far more eagles than ducks. Hooded Mergansers came once in a while to feed on small fish. Occasionally a Wood Duck or a puddle duck would make a brief appearance, but, otherwise, the Duck Hunting Gods never smiled upon me."

When we arrived at the airport, the Major took his Leg-o'-Mutton and suitcase, headed for the check-in and made a final comment. "Last year I managed to drop my first duck – a teal – and if Doc Carmichael hadn't alerted me, I wouldn't have been awake to shoot that one. In short, my young friend, the 12 ga. will stay in Philadelphia when I visit Carl Wussow. As much as I love duck hunting, I've given up on Carl Wussow's Spring Pond. From now on my attentions will be directed toward Carl's Woodcock and Ruffed Grouse."

* * * * *

Carl's nephew, Tom, lives and works in Green Bay. Like his uncle, Tom is a hunter. This year, for the first time, he would join Carl and the Major for their regular October hunt. Tom was waiting for the Major at the Austin Straubel airport. He introduced himself, loaded Peabody's gear into his pick-up and they started the trip north to Carl's cabin.

On the way, Tom told the Major how much Carl loved to hunt ducks. He told him how, for years, he had planted wild rice, duck potato and wild celery in his pot holes. Every duck in the neighborhood spends its evenings there. Tom was convinced that Canadian ducks considered Uncle Carl's pot holes to be the very best restaurants on their migratory route. Peabody's jaw dropped, but Tom was watching the road and didn't see it.

Tom chuckled about how close-mouthed Uncle Carl was about his secret duck hunting pot holes. He was sure Uncle Carl had told no one about them, excepting, of course, the Major.

Then Tom chuckled again and added how Uncle Carl usually told people to hunt his spring pond. He even built a nice blind for them even though seeing a duck on that pond was a very rare experience.

You Can't Win

"We live in a strange universe," said Major Nathaniel Peabody. "Upon careful analysis, you will discover the rules established to direct us onto the pathways of appropriate behavior are of highly questionable validity. Morality, ethics and even the simple instructions of how to lead a happy life are contradictory and confusing. Nothing is what it seems to be. What we presume to be immutable laws turn out to be quite mutable.

"Examples are legion. 'Thou shalt not kill' unless 'thou' happens to be the hangman. Stealing tens of thousands of dollars is a felony unless you happen to be a United States Senator or a member of the House of Representatives. 'Look before you leap', appears to be good advice, but remember, 'He who hesitates is lost.' 'A penny saved is a penny earned', but, still, a man can be 'penny wise and pound foolish".

It was the 27th day of September. Major Peabody and I were in Bookbinders. He was enjoying a cigar and we both had an after dinner Spanish sherry - a Tio Pepe from Jerez de la Frontera. As I recall it, we had enjoyed more than just one of them.

"Even though something leaves the impression that it is entirely clear, in fact, it may be open to many different interpretations," Peabody observed.

I immediately became suspicious. "I know what you're up to, Major," I said, "and it won't work. Your Spendthrift Trust Agreement is definitely NOT subject to a different interpretation. That document provides for the delivery of a monthly stipend on the first day of the month. It very carefully proscribes delivery before the first day of the month." I looked at my watch. "It is now thirteen minutes past eight o'clock. You can get your check in 75 hours and forty seven minutes and not a single second earlier. You know the rules."

If Peabody was disappointed, he didn't show it. He blew a smoke ring. He looked at me for a moment and then continued: "It is said there is an exception to every rule."

Now I had him. I knew, sooner or later, he would use that 'exception to every rule' ploy. I was ready for him.

"Well, Major," I answered, trying not to sound too smug, "if there is an exception to <u>every</u> rule, then that statement must be a rule. If it is a rule, then, according to its own terms, there <u>is</u> an exception to it. In other words there has to be a rule to which there is <u>no</u> exception. I'll give you an example of such a rule." I paused and enunciated clearly for emphasis and said: "There is no exception to the rule that directs the delivery of your trust stipend on the first day of the month."

Peabody effected a pained expression. "Of course, my boy, of course," he said. "I have no intention of putting you in an untenable position with your law firm by accepting an early payment." (Yes, he used the word "accepting".) "I was merely saying that rules, under certain circumstances, can quite properly be fractured, if not broken. For example - you, I am told, have adopted a rule to never bet with me. Is that right?"

The lovely Stephanie must have spilled the beans. Stephanie is my fiancé and a very beautiful, intelligent and strong minded woman. Stephanie suggested I never again make any kind of wager with Major Nathaniel Peabody. When the lovely Stephanie makes a suggestion, that suggestion must be adopted if it be your desire to continue association with her.

115

Don't misunderstand. Stephanie likes the Major. She enjoys his stories and his company. She also knows of the various times the Major has talked me into betting on a wager that, on the surface, appeared to be a safe bet. I ended up paying off on every one of those 'safe bets'.

I didn't answer the Major's question. I didn't have to. Clearly, Peabody had talked to Stephanie and he knew about her 'suggestion'.

"Don't worry, my boy," he said. "I believe I understand completely." Peabody looked at his empty glass and then at me. "I take it your firm is paying for this dinner? Entertainment of a client?" I nodded. "Well then," he said catching the eye of the waiter, "two more Tio Pepe, if you please."

Major Peabody extolled the virtues of the lovely Stephanie and emphasized our mutual good luck in finding one another. Certainly, he said, he would do nothing that might jeopardize my relationship with her. Then his eyes lit up and he said: "I have a marvelous idea. I believe you should make an exception to your rule."

"Oh", I said, feeling I was about to be invited to take my first step onto a very slippery slope.

"Undoubtedly Stephanie has suggested you refrain from betting with me because she doesn't want you disappointed in the event the gods of wagering favor me with good luck." (Good luck, my foot! Peabody doesn't leave anything to chance. He only bets on sure things.)

"That is an unmistakable sign of her affection for you," the Major explained. "Your disappointment would be too much for her to bear. Now suppose - just suppose - I were to make a bet with such extreme conditions that my opportunity to win would be practically non-existent. Suppose, further, that you won the bet. Can you imagine how pleased Stephanie would be to learn how you had outsmarted me?"

Peabody leaned back in his chair, smiling at the ingenuity of his plan. "Tomorrow morning, Doc Carmichael and I are leaving for South Dakota to help the state keep its pheasant population under control. We'll be there on the first of October when you come to deliver my check and I'll have the money to settle our bet. What do you think?"

It must have been the Tio Pepe. After receiving the assurance that the Major would not, directly or indirectly divulge even the existence of our bet to his hunting friends, we agreed on its terms. It was a joint effort. Major Peabody established half of the conditions of the wager and I named the rest. I was particularly pleased with my proposed addition of "while whistling Dixie".

* * * * *

Late in the evening of September 30, I got out of the auto I rented at the Brookings airport and entered the cabin the Major and his friends had rented for their hunting foray. Doctor Carmichael met me at the door. He was in an exuberant mood.

"Come in. Come in. Feeling well, I hope. We're all feeling very fine here - with the possible exception of Major Peabody. You brought his check? Good. He'll need it to pay off his bet. I won! First time in a couple of years."

Major Peabody sat in a well used, overstuffed chair, smiling faintly. He did not look uncomfortable and I began to feel uneasy. My discomfort increased as Doctor Carmichael explained the reason for his joy.

"Can you believe it?" he asked. "Peabody bet me fifty dollars I couldn't stand on a chair, raise one foot in the air, tap my head and rub my stomach while whistling Dixie. What's the matter? You don't look so good."

You wouldn't look so good either if you had bet five hundred dollars the Major couldn't get Carmichael to give that performance before witnesses.

Look for the Silver Lining

My law firm manages the Peabody Spendthrift Trust and two clauses in the trust document are quite clear. The trust beneficiary's interest cannot be pledged or alienated and can be delivered only on the first day of the month. The Trust beneficiary, Major Nathaniel Peabody, is quite dissatisfied with these terms.

When Major Nathaniel Peabody wasn't able to convince, cajole or threaten me into making advance payments, he studied the Trust document and then insisted the stipends be personally delivered to him on the first day of the month – regardless of where he might be found on that day. Unfortunately for me, his interpretation of the clause was deemed to be correct

The Major thought the inconvenience resulting from his demand would eventually force the Trustee (me) to ignore the Trust's terms and make early payments to him. Certainly, I was inconvenienced, but Smythe, Hauser, Engals & Tauchen was not inconvenienced in the least. The senior partner merely ordered me to make the deliveries of the Major's checks. From that day on, it became my problem.

Peabody's end-of-the-month hunting forays never took him to places like Paris, or Rome or the Greek Isles. He never gave me the pleasure of a delivery trip to such a place. On the first day of the month, the Major was more probably in the deep woods of Upper Michigan (where, he tells me, ferocious bears roamed freely) or in Arizona's Sonoran desert (where, he tells me, rattlesnakes, Gila monsters and scorpions abound).

* * * * *

On Saturday, the penultimate day of the month, I was in Philadelphia. Major Peabody was in Missouri looking for wild turkey in a remote area near a metropolis of such a size that its name didn't even appear on the maps. Of course, the Major would expect delivery of his check no later than 12:01 on Sunday morning, the first day of the ensuing month.

The turkey hunters' camp would break-up on Sunday morning and the Major would return to Philadelphia that same evening. It wouldn't have killed him to wait and let me give him his check when he was back in his apartment, but the Peabody Trust agreement said his check was to be delivered on the first day of the month and the Major insisted that meant 12:01 a.m. And that meant I had to leave for Missouri on Saturday morning.

I was not in a happy frame of mind. On Friday evening, I had a date with the lovely Stephanie. After a romantic dinner, as we drove to her condo, she snuggled up and told me Lucia di Lamermoor was being performed at the Met. She had arranged a week-end in New York City and coyly suggested I might like to accompany her. I believe she had a good idea of just how much I would have liked to accompany her.

But the flight to St. Louis left the next morning and there was no way I could find anyone to deliver the Major's check in my stead. I took a deep breath and explained it all to her. Occasionally, the lovely Stephanie is not very understanding. This was one of those times. It is true, "Heaven has no rage like love to hatred turned, nor Hell a fury like a woman scorned." I can prove it.

To make matters worse, the flight to Missouri was particularly irritating. When I arrived in St. Louis, the airline people confessed my luggage had, somehow or other, been sent to Taipei. The flight to Joplin was delayed. I got there, rumpled and disorderly in mind and spirit. I rented an auto, got lost on township roads and finally found the Major's camp after sun down and after the evening meal had been completely consumed. The hunters were at the poker table and while they concentrated on their game I managed to find some potato chips.

I was not in a good mood. I took some satisfaction in discovering Peabody, too, was not in a good mood. His accustomed end-of-the-month financial hardship was exacerbated by bad luck in the field. On Friday, the Major discovered an excellent strut zone. He watched it and the nearby roost for the entire day. Toms, larger than he had ever seen, paraded in front of him, but he held his fire.

That evening, the Major mentioned it might be interesting if each hunter invested a hundred dollars in a pool and awarded it to the one who got the largest Tom on Saturday. The other four hunters agreed.

I'm told there are nearly 400,000 wild turkeys in Missouri. On Saturday, to the Major's intense disappointment, he didn't see one of them. The various Toms that had answered his calls and paraded in front of him on Friday - well within shotgun range - had forsaken him in favor of visitations to each of his hunting companions. Coming back with an empty game bag was more than a financial loss. It was a personal embarrassment.

To add insult to injury, the poker gods refused to smile upon him. That evening the cards were very unkind. An unrelieved run of terribly bad luck plagued him. It was just after midnight when he excused himself from the table and signaled me to follow him outside the cabin.

"Well, my boy," he said to me, "life is not all beer and skittles. Did you see that last hand? I held a full house with aces up and that dentist, who has all the card sense of a mud turtle, sticks around through all the betting and draws his fourth six on the last card. It's enough to make a man resign from the church."

I was still nettled by the unfortunate experience with the lovely Stephanie. Frankly, I had little sympathy for the Major and, in fact, I will admit a certain amount of antagonism removed any pity I might normally have felt because of his run of bad luck.

"The last time I played poker with you," I responded with some smug satisfaction, "if I recall correctly, you told me adversity builds character." (It not only builds character, but also teaches caution. I promised myself I would never again play cards with the Major.)

"Do I denote a bit of edginess in your voice?" he inquired.

"Edginess? Edginess?" I answered. "Why ever would I have cause to be edgy? Unless, of course..." and I told him the details of missing an opportunity to see Lucia di Lamermoor.

"A tragedy, my boy, but, like I told you, adversity will build your character. Now then," he said, paying no further attention to my tale of woe, "I have an immediate need for three hundred and fifty dollars. You have something for me, do you not?" he said as he put out his right hand, palm up.

Revenge! Revenge! The five turkey hunters would scatter to the four winds after breakfast. The nearest village was nine miles away and it contained no banking facility. To add to Peabody's problem, it would be Sunday and the one commercial establishment in the place (a country tavern) would be closed.

I pulled the envelope from my coat pocket. "Here is your remittance, Major. As always, it is a delight to personally hand it to you. I do hope you will find some way to cash it and pay your debts before your companions leave tomorrow morning. I'm sure it would distress you if those gentlemen were to return to their homes knowing that you were unable to pay your gambling debts. But then, as you say, adversity builds character."

The Major is at his best when under pressure. His insensitivity to my problems disappeared and was replaced by sincere concern over my strained relations with the lovely Stephanie. He quickly developed a proposal to cure the breach between us.

The eloquence of Peabody's argument won me over and I agreed to lend him four hundred dollars in cash, but not before requiring him to endorse his trust check and return it to me as collateral.

* * * * *

At the end of the following month, Major Nathaniel Peabody was in the Czech Republic, participating in a driven pheasant hunt. The lovely Stephanie and I went through Customs at the airport in Prague and three days later I delivered the Major's customary monthly stipend.

Adversity

I was in Major Nathaniel Peabody's apartment. His monthly Spendthrift Trust remittance rested safely inside my jacket pocket, patiently waiting for delivery as soon as the hands of the clock told us it was after midnight and the first of the month had arrived. We sat there, silently watching the flames in the fireplace reduce the wood to coals. The Major began a one way conversation.

"When in the field," he began, "the sportsman constantly faces a serious danger. He is always aware of the potential for some unforeseen circumstance to arise and destroy the expedition. The form of such an ominous threat cannot be forecast, but there are many events that can ruin a pleasant hunt.

"The best organized adventure can be interrupted by the development of a sudden illness or some other adversity. If someone's dog decides it would be a good idea to grab a porcupine by the neck and give it a good shaking, the grouse hunt will probably be ended. The plan to spend a week on South Dakota pheasant land can be prematurely disrupted by some completely unforeseeable disaster like inadvertently bringing 16 gauge shells and a 12 gauge shotgun. An evening in a cottage on a lake known to contain ducks can become an agony if you are forced to listen to a hunter's unending whining about ammunition that doesn't hit what he aims at or the occurrence of gale force winds and sub zero temperatures.

"Adversity of any nature can destroy any hunt," Peabody concluded. "A hunter must always be alert. Let's say someone brings a newspaper into camp. Immediate action is required. It is important to understand media financial success is dependant upon reporting stories of dreadful catastrophes and frightful calamities. Hunters tend to be a simple and naïve lot. If they are left to their own devices, they may read the newspaper and actually believe what is printed in it. If so, an atmosphere of dejection will surely pervade the camp and it will no longer be a happy place.

"Don't get me wrong, young man. I'm not one of those in the vast majority of the population who are convinced the newspapers are worthless rags. The Supreme Being did not create newspapers without intending some valuable purpose for them. Newspapers are useful in starting fires in the camp wood stove. In addition, newspapers be cut into four or five inch strips and rolled up. Appropriate sized lengths may then be torn off and used for a worthwhile purpose if someone forgot to bring the toilet tissue. One must remember, however, that newspaper ink will leave a black smudge on the Gluteus Maximus.

"Another danger is represented by soggy playing cards. When confronted with such an outrage, one must not dissolve into a mass of blubbering hysteria. If he is to defeat adversity, the poker player must keep his wits about him. He must face up to the challenge and exercise the most careful of attentions to avoid misdealing. Misdeals can result in accusations of incompetence and fist fights. Fists fights, if allowed to get out of hand, could destroy the friendly camaraderie necessary to all hunting camps.

"An unforeseen death is yet another example of an adversity that could distract from the joys of the occasion. If a man dies in the middle of a grouse hunt, his camp-mates may become mildly depressed and forego the following morning's hunt.

"The failure to deal with adversity has destroyed more hunts than the failure to bring insect repellant to the springtime Canadian tundra. The experienced hunter is quick to recognition potentially disruptive situations. He is conditioned to resolutely confront and overcome whatever camp-destroying danger that might arise."

The Major rattled the ice cubes in his glass. I performed my function and re-filled it. Peabody sipped, nodded his approval and then continued his story.

"Last year I was invited to travel to the southern shore of Hudson Bay to hunt geese and waterfowl. I knew two of the three other men in our group. They were experienced hunters.

"Steve and Mike and I had developed the kind of special relationship enjoyed only by men who have hunted together or shared the same cell for a number of years. The fourth member of the group - Henry Something-Or-Other - was unknown to me.

"After three or four changes of airplane, we landed at an abandoned Canadian air force base at Winisk near the shores of Hudson Bay and were driven to our base camp. That's when adversity raised its ugly head. Steve, Mike and my shotguns arrived safely, but Henry's weapon did not. It was probably in the unclaimed baggage section of the Timmins or the Moosonee airport. Being an experienced hunter, Steve immediately recognized how the man's misfortune could have a dampening affect on the pleasure of our shoot. He took immediate action.

"He put his arm around Henry's shoulder, demanded he stop his whimpering and tried to comfort him. He told him it could have been much worse - it could have been his, or Mike's or my shotgun that had been left behind. In spite of Steve's friendly attempt to help him, the man continued to snivel. Steve was forced to turn and walk away in order to avoid having to listen to his miserable complaining. It became clear that Henry was unable to deal with adversity.

"Mike, too, tried to deal with the danger resulting from Henry's bad luck. He convinced one of our Cree Indian guides to let Henry rent his twelve ga. The guide's shotgun was a 1930's vintage humpbacked Remington version of the Browning automatic. The weapon's rust and split but duct taped stock proved it had seen substantial service. The rental figure was a bit high and was phrased in US, not Canadian, dollars."

Peabody sipped from his drink and slowly shook his head as he considered Henry's lack of appreciation. "You just can't please some people," he said. "Can you believe it? Henry complained about the rental price. Privately, Mike asked me if he should reduce Henry's cost by the twenty percent commission the overjoyed guide gave him for negotiating such a favorable rental agreement. Of course, I told him 'No'. It would have been unworthy of Mike to change the terms of the contract by sacrificing his own well-earned commission.

"The owner of the gun decided to be Henry's personal guide. He wanted to make sure his Remington was not abused. He stuck to Henry just like the pine pitch that filled the cracks in the boat's seat impregnated and stuck to the seat of Henry's $275.00 Serac Gore-Tex nylon hunting pants. As is the case with all complainers, Henry voiced his unhappiness whenever he sat down and was stuck to whatever he sat down on.

"The guide didn't speak much English and Henry hadn't had the foresight to learn the Cree language. Communication between the two of them was tenuous at best. I'm sure the guide tried to tell Henry that members of the Cree Nation were not subject to the Canadian duck hunting regulation requiring plugged automatics and three shell limits. Henry had often fired five shots at retreating ducks and had re-loaded the

Remington many times. He knew the weapon was not plugged.

"Had he learned Cree, Henry would have been able to tell his guide why he desperately tried to hand the weapon to him when he saw the Mounted Policeman coming toward him to check for game violations. Given the communication problem, you can't blame the guide for thinking Henry was trying to reduce the cost in the hourly rental contract by handing him the gun. The Cree shoved the Remington back to him every time Henry tried to put it in his hands.

"In another effort to soften the effects of adversity, Steve, Mike and I commiserated with Henry about the exceptionally heavy fine he had to pay. Nevertheless, Henry was inconsolable. His incessant whimpering and complaining nearly destroyed the hunt. It would have been ruined for lesser men, but Steve, Mike and I knew how to overcome adversity.

"We paid no attention to Henry. We ignored him during the daylight hours and, when back in camp, we avoided him as men in the Middle Ages would avoid a leper. One dark and stormy night, we threw him out of our tent. He had to move in with the guide where he was able to whine and complaint at length. (The reason the Cree guide never bothered to learn English became apparent. He just smiled, said nothing, and went to sleep.)

"This is an excellent example of how experienced hunters like Steve and Mike and me will not allow adversity to spoil our hunt."

Surprise

I've tried to condition myself never to be surprised by anything Major Nathaniel Peabody says or does. It has not been an easy task. I've been at it for years and there were times when I believed I had succeeded, but I was always wrong.

I was truly surprised when the Major announced he was going to attend a party organized by the members of the Desmond County Woodcock Watchers Protective Society. The Society is widely known for its violently anti-hunter and anti-gun activities. Among other propositions, each year the DCWWPS sponsors legislation designed to declare the hunting of Woodcock to be a crime requiring capitol punishment. I could think of no rational reason why Peabody would agree to be present at one of the Society's functions.

When I cautiously wondered why he was going to the meeting, my surprise was magnified to incredulity. Peabody advised me the Society was so-named because it was dedicated to the protection of Woodcock Watchers and that he was interested in meeting kindred spirits. Just like the members of the Society, he, too, was an avid Woodcock Watcher. He carefully watched for them when he was carrying a shotgun in the autumn woods and lowlands.

The reason for the Major's erroneous interpretation of the Society's purposes and activities became apparent to me when he said Doctor Carmichael had arranged for his attendance at the meeting. Doctor Carmichael has a peculiar sense of humor. I suspected this was his way of getting a degree of pay-back for some outrage the Major had directed toward him. I could understand how the doctor would mislead him for the pure joy of watching the Major's extreme discomfort when, surrounded by Society members, he discovered their true objectives.

Peabody asked me if I would drive him to the party site. Of course, I immediately agreed. This was one party I wouldn't miss for all the tea in China (and in India and in England, too). Frankly, I looked forward to watching him try to control his temper and avoid the crude and combative comments he would normally be expected to make when he learned of the Society's enmity toward bird hunters in general and to Woodcock hunters in particular.

When we arrived at the home of Mr. Frederick Goodfellow, the president of the Society, the party was in full swing. I half expected a veritable explosion when those in attendance discovered a bird hunter in their midst. I stayed close to the Major, hoping to restrain him if he appeared ready to engage in a fist fight. The first test came at the hors d'oeuvres table, I found myself in a position where I had to introduce Major Peabody to our host. My fears evaporated when it became apparent that Frederick Goodfellow knew nothing about Peabody or his obsession with shotgun hunting.

Those fears quickly re-appeared when Goodfellow bemoaned the shooting of Woodcock and characterized all hunters as uncivilized, cruel and bloodthirsty criminals who should be arrested, tried, convicted and sentenced to death by firing squad. I held my breath as Peabody curled his upper lip, just as a pit bulldog might do. Somehow, he managed to control himself. In the face of such a set of particularly obscene comments, the Major limited himself to emitting a few unintelligible gurgling sounds which Goodfellow interpreted as an indication of full agreement with his statements.

During the rest of the afternoon, Peabody showed few

further signs of needing restraint. I watched as he mingled and chatted with the members and though often provoked, only once did he temporarily lose his composure. I noticed a rather large, tweedy lady, wearing flat heeled, brown walking shoes and a severe hairdo. She had been surreptitiously watching the Major.

Finally, she swooped down and cornered him. It looked like trouble to me. I shouldered my way through the crowd and to the Major's side. I got there in time to overhear her introduce herself, proclaimed her widowhood and, rather coyly, I thought, questioned him about the sex life of the Woodcock.

The lady listened attentively as Peabody described the electric-type "peeent, peeent" call of the male birds as they circled, flying high in the dusk-time skies. He explained how the birds tumbled to an open area on the ground and how the females surreptitiously watched them, made their selections, and then swooped down and cornered them.

As he spoke, the lady studied the Major in a speculative manner. She responded to his discourse by asking if he were married. Peabody's eyes opened to their widest. He stepped back half a pace. I believe he panicked. It took him a few moments to compose himself. Then he answered.

"Yes, Madame, I am married. I have two wives. One does the cooking and the other takes care of the housekeeping." Then he studied her in a speculative manner and asked; "How are you at washing clothes?" The lady's eyes opened to their widest. She stepped back half a pace. I believe she panicked. Regaining her composure, she excused herself and went to hunt in more productive terrain.

As the afternoon came to a close, the Society members dispersed and I searched for Major Peabody. He had behaved admirably. He had been proper and civil and even polite in his conversations with the enemy. When I found him, he was chatting pleasantly with Frederick Goodfellow. I heard the last part of the conversation.

"Why, Major Peabody," Goodfellow gushed, "that's very nice of you – comparing me to a Woodcock. It is such a noble bird. It lives free in nature's wonderland. In spite of the dangers it faces from owls, foxes, those terrible hunters and other equally nasty predators, it survives and maintains its dignity. Thank you for your most considerate compliment."

As we drove back to Philadelphia, I couldn't help but think of the extraordinary events of the day: Peabody voluntarily remaining in the very midst of his sworn antagonists; Peabody, nevertheless, refusing to adopt either verbal or physical assault tactics against the enemy; and, Peabody actually complimenting Frederick Goodfellow. The Major explained that later wonderment.

"I hope Mr. Goodfellow will take the trouble of studying the Woodcock," he said. "If he does, he will find the bird's eyes are placed near the back of its head, not close to its beak. He'll learn the Woodcock's ears are below and in front of its eyes, not above and behind them. He'll also discover the Woodcock's brain is located near the bottom of its skull and is upside down. Then perhaps, he'll understand I was not complimenting him. I was trying to tell him that he, too, had his head on backwards."

* * * * *

A few days later, Major Peabody and Doc Carmichael enjoyed a successful day in the field. The sun was setting when the two hunters returned to Major Peabody's apartment.

"A great day, Nate," said the doctor.

"Yes it was," Peabody answered. "Come on up and have a

drink or two."

"Certainly, if you promise not to try to give me the blended stuff someone passed off on you."

"I only offer that to people I don't like," Peabody answered and he took his Leg o' Mutton gun case and a dead Woodcock from the back of Carmichael's vehicle.

Carmichael wrinkled his nose and, in a tone of disbelief asked; "You're not going to eat that, are you?"

"Of course not, Doc. I'm going to have it mounted. I'll send it to that   Goodfellow guy. It's the least I can do for him. After all, he's the one who told me where his bird watchers found the highest concentrations of Woodcock. He gave me reports on three more likely spots. We'll try one of them next Saturday."

Save the Environment

A medical emergency arose during one of Major Nathaniel Peabody's grouse hunting expeditions. A young hunter, unaccustomed to the dangers of entering the woods without appropriate provisions, received an urgent call of nature and found he had neglected to bring any form of paper with him. In his confusion he wiped with a handful of poison ivy. Miles from modern medical services, the poor fellow had to resort to the partial relief afforded by a river mud poultice. He had to apply it himself. None of his fellow hunters would volunteer for the job.

That evening as the men sat around the campfire (except the young hunter, who preferred to stand or lean against a tree), Major Peabody rattled the ice cubes in his empty glass and, while one of his companions found the single malt Scotch and performed the re-fill ceremony, the Major began a discourse designed to enlighten his shotgunning associates.

"The historians tell us," he began, "that toilet paper was first made in China in 1391. The sheets were two feet by three feet in size and only the Emperor was entitled to use them. Federal Government records identify Mr. Seth Wheeler as the man who invented perforated toilet paper. He received Patent #117355 on July 25, 1871. You will all recall this earth shattering event occurred 22 years after the 1849 California gold rush when thousands of people hurried across the prairies to strike it rich in the new El Dorado.

"That trip was a rough and rugged one for those pioneers

and a rough and rugged life awaited them on the West Coast. At the time of the gold rush, you see, there was no perforated toilet paper. How could those hearty pioneers have survived? The answer, friends, is simple. They eschewed the use of poison ivy and, instead, used corn cobs. Of course, they first removed all of the corn kernels.

"The 20th century development of paper technology by companies like Kimberly Clark, Scott and Northern Tissue (which advertised: "Not a splinter in a roll") popularized toilet tissue in the 1920s and 30s. What with the subsequent world-wide population explosion, huge volumes of the stuff are now annually produced.

"There are those who are convinced the toilet paper industry represents a serious threat to the universe. Certain Hollywood intellectuals are pushing a program designed to save humanity from the evils of toilet paper." The Major looked at the young man leaning against the tree as he sometimes squirmed and grimaced. "Don't worry, young man," Peabody said. "Nobody is suggesting the substitution of poison ivy. Hollywood has something else in mind and, I understand, the proposal is gaining traction in California. It may result in yet another of those peculiar California laws.

"There's an awful lot of used West Coast toilet paper going down the drain every day. Let's conservatively presume the average Californian uses five sheets of toilet paper per operation and produces three operations per day. That's 5,475 sheet per person per year - 5,490 during leap years. Since the population of California is estimated to be 336,500,000, that means in California alone, about one trillion, 742 billion, 337, million, 500 thousand sheets of used toilet paper go into the California sewerage system every year. And, I haven't counted the paper used by California's undocumented and uncounted illegals.

"There are many well intentioned Hollywood types who have never worn out a pair of boots in their lifetime and wouldn't know Mother Nature if she knocked them down and sat on them. Nevertheless, they should be applauded for their good intentions to protect the old girl. The entertainment world intellectuals are now preaching the advantages of using only one square of toilet paper during each of our regular daily lower intestinal exercises. The benefits of their program, we are informed, are numerous.

"A lot of trees have to be cut down to produce one and three-quarters trillion sheets of toilet tissue. By reducing usage from five to one sheet per evacuation, in California alone, at least one trillion 400 billion sheets of toilet paper will be saved. By using only one sheet instead of five, Californian's yearly production of one and 3/4 trillion used toilet paper sheets can be reduced to a mere 350 million. By eliminating the need for so much paper, a lot of trees will no longer have to be cut. The rain forests will be saved.

"Saving the rain forests is not the only environmentally responsible result of that proposal. If the one sheet rule becomes mandatory in that State, the toilet paper industry will be forced to reduce their destruction of California's beautiful forests by 80 percent. As a result, thousand of miles of woodsy bicycle and walking trails can be constructed for California folks to use for healthy exercise as they bicycle and jog and commune with nature.

"Still another benefit will occur. Given new prime forest habitat, the mountain lion population will expand. With a larger and healthier mountain lion population, the animal can be taken off the Endangered Species List. Moreover, the people who use California's new bicycle and walking trails will become a source of food for the increased number of marauding mountain lions. California's terrible overpopulation problem could be held in check by hungry cougars.

"To be fair about it, Hollywood's mandatory one sheet proposal does nothing to solve a related and equally serious environmental problem. Let's say each California toilet flush carries one and a half gallons of water. At three flushes per day, that's 1,642.5 gallons per California inhabitant per year. Considering the entire population of the State, somewhere around five and a quarter billion gallons of West Coast water per year is going down the drain.

"On a good day, Lake Tahoe contains 22,800 cubic meters of water. A thousand gallons of water is equal to about a cubic meter. 22,800 flushings are equal to about 13,300 cubic meters of water. If Californians got their flushing water from Lake Tahoe, 58 percent of the volume of water contained in the lake would go down the tubes each year. What a frightful cause for alarm for the Hollywood types who have property on Lake Tahoe.

"The one sheet program does nothing to reduce the total number of California toilet flushes. Since the water and the paper eventually end up in the salty ocean, the Hollywood program does little to save humanity from the terrible consequences of the slow but inevitable destruction of the State's entire fresh water supply. According to the environmentalists, when good drinking water runs out, Californians will all have to face the terror of having to buy and drink California wines."

Peabody stared down at his feet and said to himself. "What we really need is a way to save both the world's forests and the world's water supply." Then he brightened as the answer came to him. "The 49ers provide the answer. Not the football team, I refer to the rugged 49ers - the ones who came across the prairies in covered wagons.

Hollywood types can emulate their pioneer ancestors and

use corn cobs. They require no flushing. Changing the Hollywood one sheet proposal to a one corn cob proposal will do away with all toilet paper, saving even more of the rain forests. By eliminating the need to flush, Californians will keep the world's water supply in a pure and pristine condition."

Peabody concluded his lecture. "The disposal of used corn cobs," he said, "presents no problem. Since they are biodegradable, they can be deposited in front of Hollywood's Malibu Beach homes, providing a natural barrier to protect against beach erosion." Then he looked up and was disappointed to find his friends had lost interest in his environmentalism and wandered off. Only the young man remained. He was preoccupied with rubbing his hind side against the tree.

A Christmas Carol

It was mid-December. There was a light covering of snow on the ground - just enough to require Philadelphia's soot and grime to color it black. The skies were gray, too. Nevertheless, it was the season to be jolly. Soon Smythe, Hauser, Engels and Tauchen would announce the firm's office Christmas party and gifts would be exchanged. Soon, the regular end-of-year bonuses would be distributed. In spite of the gloom of the weather, the spirit of the holiday was making its presence known. Secretaries began covering their desks with festive decoration and I found myself developing the "ho-ho-ho" attitude toward everything.

I was full of cheer and good spirits and I thought about Major Nathaniel Peabody. Though his Spendthrift Trust remittance wasn't due for delivery until January 1 – another 19 days – I presumed he would, nevertheless, be caught up in the pleasantries attending the Christmas and New Year holidays. Then I remembered Peabody's nearest relatives were separated from him both by geography and by temperament. It occurred to me the Major would spend the holidays alone in this apartment. It would not be a joyous occasion for him. On the contrary, it would be a lonely time.

I could understand why the Major might not greet the season with unbridled joy. I was happy, but he, in all probability, was sad. Somehow, I felt guilty. To erase that feeling, I decided to give him a special present. I visited a tobacconist and made a substantial investment in a box of H.

Upmann six ring cigars. The next stop was the Major's apartment. I knocked at his door.

At first there was no response. After the third try, the door opened and, without as word of greeting, Peabody let me in. "Good afternoon, Major," I said. I smiled, in accordance with the custom dictated by the holiday spirit. "You're looking well." Peabody remained silent. "A very happy Yule time tiding to you, Major," I said and reached out to hand him the present.

Peabody really didn't look well. His eyes had lost their sparkle. His expression seemed fixed and empty. Without comment of any sort, he stared at me for a few seconds and then took the gaily wrapped box of cigars from my hand. He placed it, unopened, on the table beside the winged back chair next to his fireplace. As I suspected, the Christmas season had not been a happy time for him. Clearly, he needed cheering up.

"You look just a bit depressed," I said to him. "And at this time of year, too. It's unforgivable, Major. Just look around you. People are shopping and full of the Christmas spirit. Children have their noses pressed against the toy store windows, wondering what old Santa will bring them. Ha, ha, ha."

Then Peabody spoke for the first time. It was a quotation from Richard III. "How weary, stale, flat and unprofitable seem to me all the uses of this world," he said. "Fie on't. Oh, fie. 'Tis an unweeded garden that grows to seed; things rank and gross in nature possess it merely."

That Shakespearean quote convinced me Peabody's depression was a bit deeper than I had suspected. He must have been sitting there for some time. The ice in his drink had melted and the liquid at the bottom of his glass was uncharacteristically colorless. He made no attempt to rattle the non-existent ice cubes – the usual method he had adopted to receive a re-fill. He simple handed me the glass, saying: "Have one yourself."

I did. I put a little extra Scotch in the one I brought to him. I thought it would be easy to bring some joy into his life, so I brightly suggested: "If your busy social calendar happens to be open, why don't we visit Bookbinders tonight and see if their rack of lamb is as good as advertised?"

Peabody wasn't tempted. "No," he answered. "I just don't feel up to it."

Now, I was really worried. I was sure the Major knew my present was a box of cigars by the weight and size of the package, but he didn't bother to open it. The unattended single malt Scotch and water was an additional signal of his distress. His refusal to enjoy one of his favorite meals at one of his favorite restaurants was further proof of depression. He had to be pulled out of his funk. I decided on the direct approach.

"Come on, Major," I said to him. "I know Christmas can be a sad time – especially if you're alone. It's tough when you are all by yourself and surrounded by the signs of the holidays, by televised Christmassy programs, by the carols, by the store windows, by the smiles and the greetings of friends and strangers. It's only natural for a wistful yearning for something lost or unrecoverable to enter your thoughts. Nostalgia can be sweet or bittersweet or sad. It all depends on what you make of it. Like the song says: You got to accentuate the positive, eliminate the negative, latch on to the affirmative and don't mess with Mr. In-Between."

"You're probably right," Peabody answered quietly, "but it's easier to give advice than it is to take it. You've got the lovely Stephanie and your office associates. You've lived here all your life and have your circle of friends. All of you have families for Christmas dinners and gatherings around the

Christmas tree." Peabody produced a small derisive 'humpf' sound. "All I've got are relatives in Virginia who don't approve of me. Would you suggest I visit them?" he questioned in a somewhat laconic manner.

"I don't know what to suggest," I answered. "I do know this is not a time for you to sit in your apartment thinking lonely thoughts. It's a time when you should be with friends. Surely you have some friends."

* * * * *

Doc Carmichael got out of the pit and stretched. He had a good day and he was happy. Speckled Belly and Blue geese were in abundance. Canadas and Snows completed the birds that joined with the millions of other waterfowl at their winter staging area in Mexico's northeastern Gulf coast. The guide picked up the fallen geese and they headed toward the vehicle that would carry them back to the lodge.

They detoured past another blind and the guide added more geese to his burden as Major Peabody got out of his pit. "You must be getting old, Doc," the Major said to him. "I saw you miss a couple of easy shots."

"I don't recall missing any easy shots," was Carmichael's response. "I don't even remember missing some very difficult shots. I do, however, vividly recall a Speckled Belly that tried to land inside your pit. If he hadn't flared at the last moment, I believe he would have knocked your hat off."

"I remember that one, too, Doc. I was distracted. I was chuckling over how easy it was to con my attorney into delivering my January Trust remittance over two weeks early – just in time to be able to join you on this hunt. I knew I had him when he said: 'It's a time when you should be with friends.'

"Tomorrow, let's go for ducks on one of those fresh water lakes."

Ground Swatting

In autumn, when the sun goes down in Michigan's Upper Peninsula, the chill in the evening air is a warning of the all-too-soon appearance of snow, gray skies and the icy winds of winter. The pine and fir and spruce stolidly insist on retaining their dark green, but deciduous hardwoods dress up in yellows and reds and the tamarack begin to think about turning orange. It is the time of year when coveys of Ruffed Grouse scatter and men pick up shotguns and go into the woods to look for them.

Major Nathaniel Peabody was there, seated with fellow hunters around a blazing camp fire. He moved his camp stool a few inches back from the fire. It was only a slight change of position, but it was enough to alter the way the surrounding air moved. As a result, the smoke changed its direction and now blew into the eyes of the men seated on the opposite side of the fire.

Doc Carmichael was finishing his story. "So the kid says: 'You're not going to shoot that grouse while he's running on the ground, are you, Grandfather?' and the old man, with the barrel of his shotgun pointing out the car window, says: 'No, but if the little s o b ever stops I'm going to let him have it." Laughter ensued even though the hunters in Peabody's circle considered a man who would shoot a bird on the ground to be worse than a liberal.

Peabody pulled a branch from the fire and lit a cigar with its glowing end. "Charlie," he said, "As long as you're up, will you do something about this?" He rattled the ice in his empty glass. Charlie wasn't standing but he got up from the block of wood he used as a chair and complied with the Major's request.

The Major took the drink Charlie proffered. He thanked him, sipped, nodded his approval and commented on the doctor's story.

"The custom of refusing to ground swat a bird has been around nearly as long as the Second Amendment," he said. "It is my understanding that on the first Sunday of every October, one of your U P clergymen delivers a sermon entitled: 'Thou Shalt Not Ground Swat'. He insists it is the Eleventh Commandment. I'm not too sure of that, but I am convinced it is one of the provisions contained within the Magna Carta. Nevertheless, I believe the time has come for us to consider the rejection of our own long standing practice of outlawing ground swatting."

Reaction was immediate. Comments flew through the cool night air. "He's gone mad." "Surely, you jest." "I've suspected it for some time. He's senile." "No more for him, Charlie. He's drunk. Cut him off."

"Be serious Major," one of the hunters said. "The grouse have enough problems with their population cycles, thick crusted snow in the wintertime, foxes and pine martens. If we began shooting birds on the ground, there wouldn't be many grouse left in the county."

Peabody thought for a moment before joining in debate. "There is no evidence that hunting has been an important factor in the extinction of any bird. And don't tell me hunters finished off the Passenger Pigeon. It was a disease that did that job. A look at the reasons for extinctions is instructive. The Great Auk, the Dodo and the Moa come to mind.

"The Dodo was not driven to extinction by hunters. It was as big as a huge turkey, but, unable to fly, it offered no wing shooting challenge to the sportsman. Moreover, it had drab plumage and its meat was tough. Women wouldn't buy hats made with its feathers and it didn't taste good. Sportsmen, commercial interests and hungry people had no reason to kill it. The Dodo was finished off by the animals that were introduced to the island of Mauritius by Europeans.

"The Moa," he continued, "was a monstrously big wingless bird. It grew to a height of twelve feet. Unable to fly, wing shooting bird hunters were not involved in its extinction. I will, however, admit ground-swatters may have helped them down the road to oblivion. Presumably, the bird was good to eat. The aborigines of New Zealand, the Maoris, killed it off. Shotgunners, I hasten to point out, were not involved. For all practical purposes, the Moa was extinct before firearm carrying sportsmen appeared in New Zealand.

"The Great Auk is yet another example. It couldn't fly and wing shooters weren't interested in it. Sailors and business people clubbed the Great Auk into the history books sometime around 1844. It was a good supplement to the usual eighteenth and nineteenth century sailing vessel food menus. The Great Auk's feathers and oil were valuable commercial commodities. These were the factors causing the demise of the species..

"Incidentally, in the North Atlantic, the Great Auk was called 'penguin'. When it became extinct in that part of the world, the name was transferred to a completely unrelated bird common to the Southern Hemisphere. That penguin can't fly. It uses its scaled wings as paddles and some of them, like that flightless New Zealand apteryx, the Kiwi, build their nests underground. A bird that can't fly and lives underground can hardly attract the attention of a bird hunter. If the penguin ever becomes extinct, our eco-terrorist friends will have to blame the sea leopard or climatic change as the cause."

Charlie and the others were silent. They didn't know what

to say. Only a few weeks earlier, Peabody had roundly chastised a man who proposed: "Let's do some road hunting tomorrow." Now, he actually seemed serious about his ground swatting suggestion

Doc Carmichael was the first to speak. "I suppose I can agree that bird hunters have never seriously contributed to the extinction of any species but all hunters are part of the universal fraternity known as 'Sportsmen'. What possible sport can there be in opening a car window and blasting away at a bird standing motionless in the middle of the road?

"Ruffed Grouse is my favorite meal," said another hunter, "but I don't like it well enough to ground swat one of them."

"Maybe you can build a box trap, bait it with seeds and catch them that way," Charlie sarcastically muttered. "You won't have to buy shotgun shells."

Peabody paused and again rattled the ice cubes in his now empty glass. Charlie didn't bother to look at him. Instead, he said. "You know where the Scotch is, Major, Get your own drink,"

Peabody showed no reaction. He merely smiled and continued his argument. "My suggestion," he said, speaking slowly and looking at each of his companions, "was motivated solely by my universally recognized charitable nature."

Heads snapped erect. Sounds like: "Whaaaat?" and "I told you. He's lost it" and "Amazing" were heard. Disregarding the confusion and rising clamor, Peabody continued.

"I must express my surprise," he said, as he tried to blow a smoke ring. The attempt was unsuccessful because he couldn't smile and keep his lips in the form needed to blow the ring. "After witnessing your collective display of incompetence during today's shoot, I'm surprised at your antagonism to the potential of allowing ground swatting. None of you can hit a bird in the air. I thought you'd all be pleased with a rule change that would allow you to bring home a grouse and lie about how you got it."

Charlie again arose from his seat and began to pour out a Scotch and water for the Major while the others, realizing they had been had, shut their eyes and slowly shook their heads back and forth.

Vengeance Is Mine Saith Peabody

It was mid-July. "Summertime and the livin' is easy." So goes the old Gershwin tune. During July in Philadelphia, whenever one is away from the air-conditioning, the livin' can be hot, sweaty and generally uncomfortable. In spite of living in an air conditioned apartment, Major Nathaniel Peabody is apt to be a bit depressed during the time of summer heat - unless, of course, there is a hunting expedition in the offing.

In July, the northern hemisphere bird hunting seasons are mostly closed. The cooler drier Central America highlands are a good place for a hunter. The prospects of a trip to a moderate climate where dogs and shotguns are not viewed with alarm could have lifted the Major's spirits and changed his attitude from melancholy to smiling, charming affability.

However, Peabody had already used his July Trust installment by replacing his well-used hunting clothing with new Gore Tex boots, brush pants, a hunting jacket and all the other hunting paraphernalia that struck his fancy. As a result of those expenditures, the Major's cash position had been reduced to a point approaching absolute zero.

When he complained about his situation, I had to again remind him of the provision in the Peabody Trust that banned any kind of advance payment. There would be no hunting expedition to break the muggy monotony of this July. Peabody couldn't afford a trip to Wilmington, let alone to the kind of back-of-the-moon locations he and his shotgun seemed to prefer.

With no way to escape Philadelphia until the arrival of his August stipend, I suspected Peabody would be in a seriously depressed state. I also suspected a dinner followed by cigars and brandy would lift his spirits. I phoned to extend an invitation to him. My suspicion of his frame of mind was immediately and fully confirmed. The Major usually answers the phone with the words: "This is Peabody". This time he simply grumbled: "What do you want." The emphasis was on the "you".

"This is your friendly attorney, I responded.

"Well?" he questioned, rather gruffly.

After I explained the purpose of my call, the Major's tone changed only slightly. "That's very kind of you, young man," he answered and, without pause, told me: "I know just the place. It's called the Gemutlickheit. In German it translates roughly as 'good time'." He repeated the words "good time" and gave a scornful snort that emphasized his unhappy attitude.

The silent and subdued trip between the Major's apartment and the restaurant was something akin to following a hearse on its trip to a cemetery. Once seated in the Gemutlickheit, the Major ordered ox joint and beer for both of us. As soon as it was served, he attacked it with obvious relish, informing me that it was of superlative quality.

I found that information to be of questionable accuracy. My stomach rebelled against the heavier Teutonic fare. Peabody called me "dainty" when he saw how carefully I separated the meat from the bone and its surrounding layers of fat and ox skin. "Eat the whole thing," he told me. "It's not only delicious. It's good for you."

Peabody's suggestion did nothing to change my opinion of either the food's good taste or its health value. It wasn't only the ox joint. The associated vegetables were equally unattractive to me. Cabbage gives me gas and the dumplings reminded me of solid tennis balls. I knew my stomach would disapprove and show its displeasure.

Nevertheless, I did the best I could to follow Peabody's suggestion. I knew I would pay a heavy price for it, but I ate the whole thing. I had invited Peabody to dinner for the purpose of restoring his cheerful personality and I intended to succeed. I saw signs of Peabody's mood beginning to improve. If I showed how much I disliked the ox joint, its fat and its skin - not to mention the cabbage and the tennis balls - I feared I would destroy the pleasant atmosphere of the dinner and Peabody might slip back into his gloomy dejection.

During the dinner, Peabody's disposition showed continued improvement. He enjoyed the German cuisine. His mood became increasingly cheerful and he began to smile. His conversation showed signs of animation. He was returning to his old self. In spite of my own growing discomfort and abdominal pressures, I was pleased, nearly to the point of smug satisfaction. I had cleverly manipulated the Major out of his mild depression.

I choked everything down and managed (barely) to keep it down. I even found myself unable to refuse Peabody's suggestion that we celebrate the German meal with an after-dinner drink of German Schnapps. Let me warn the uninitiated. Schnapps is a liquid that should be used to remove paint from automobiles and nothing else. The soft tissues of the alimentary canal were never designed to come in contact with it. While the shock of it (thankfully) removed some of my memory, I seem to recall Peabody laughing when he saw my repeated gurgling and tearful reactions to it.

The evening and my discomfort progressed. The cabbage produced the effect it usually has on me. My unhappy stomach rumbled its displeasure over the contents I had provided. Then my intestines took over and I did so want to get back to my apartment for the Pepto-Bismol, Maalox, Rolaids, Gas-X (especially the Gas-X) and other remedies that crowd my medicine cabinet. Peabody disregarded my veiled pleas to call it an evening.

As the minutes slipped by, my discomfort turned into agony. Peabody, however, had fully recovered his jovial good humor. He blew smoke rings, he happily chattered away and he ordered more Schnapps. I drank some only because of Peabody's urgings. To add to my own discomfort, Peabody recounted stories about encounters with ferocious bears, stopping only when I reminded him of how much I feared them.

Then he talked about how otherwise nice dogs would suddenly and viciously attack people who they sensed were afraid of them. I thought of the many times I had to pass snarling and barking dogs when jogging or delivering Peabody's checks in some woodland location. Those thoughts added to my distress.

The Major was enjoying himself. I wasn't enjoying anything. I sat at the table, silent and increasingly tortured by a combination of ox joint, cabbage, tennis balls, gas and thoughts of fearsome animals. It was only with great difficulty that on more than one occasion, I got him to change the subject.

You have no idea of the magnitude of my relief when the Major got the waiter's attention, pointed at me and called for the check. On the drive back to his apartment, my head ached, my stomach ached and I couldn't seem to forget Peabody's descriptions of snarling bears, vicious wolverines and fanged dogs. I was dejected, dispirited and despondent. Peabody, however, was quite cheerful.

When I parked in front of Peabody's apartment, my primary interest was to return to my apartment and to my medicine cabinet ASAP. The Major didn't immediately leave my car. He took a few minutes to inform me that I would do well to acknowledge the existence of the hunting gods.

"They protect hunters," he explained. Then he looked at me in a fashion that can only be described as accusatory. "Attorneys are quite apt to cause trouble for hunters," he said. "They prosecute them for trespass. They sue them just because they don't pay their bills. They cause them to be fined for forgetting to buy licenses and create all sorts of mischief.

"Can you believe it? Some of them have dedicated themselves to drafting Spendthrift Trusts with the most offensive of terms. Lawyers are the ones who are responsible for making honest men sweat in Philadelphia in July rather than allowing them to enjoy a duck or dove hunt in the more pleasant climates.

"Sometimes the hunter gods visit retribution on such men in the form of headaches and gastric distress. Whenever I witness that retribution taking place, I remember there is justice on the universe and my spirits are revived."

October Song

During the first month of the Ruffed Grouse season. Major Peabody and Doctor Carmichael rented a vehicle and left the Green Bay airport. After a brief stop for necessary provisions (a cooler, lots of ice for libations, single malt Scotch whisky, crackers and both Camembert and Brie soft cheeses), they headed north. Soon they were in a forested section of Oconto County. Both men silently watched the Wisconsin fall forest as they drove to Jeff's cabin on the South Branch.

The roadside sumac were mostly bright red and the maple trees were showing off. Some of them preferred chrome yellow. Others adorned themselves with rusty brown-red foliage. A few selected a shiny, bright red autumn dress. The pople had begun to lose their crown leaves but most of them were still a kind of muted yellow from top to bottom. Sunlight found its way through the branches of the trees and revealed the earth tones of the forest floor. The darker greens of the pine and the spruce and the balsam accentuated all of the other colors.

In autumn, the northern deciduous woods are a sight to behold. Doc Carmichael appreciated the scenery. Peabody was not in the best of spirits and Carmichael tried to raise them by drawing attention to the beautiful autumn day. He broke the silence. "Just look at those leaves," he said.

"Yes," Peabody answered sullenly. "Just look at the damned things. When a bird flushes, it won't take more than three seconds before it disappears behind them. I don't know if

I can shoot that fast." He thought for a moment. Then he snorted. "When a bird flushes," he repeated. "I should say: 'If a bird flushes'. Jeff says the grouse are nearing the bottom of their cycle. We'll be lucky if we see one."

The Major was disappointed. He had looked forward to another of the great grouse hunts he usually enjoyed on his early October expeditions, but the prospects for this hunt were not particularly favorable. First, instead of spending an entire week with his Wisconsin friends, Doc Carmichael's surgery schedule limited them to a short two day hunt. Second, it looked like there weren't too many birds this year.

The only thing Doc Carmichael had accomplished was to draw Peabody's attention to the thick foliage and further depress him. The men lapsed into a silence that ended only after they turned down the two rutted trail that ended at the cabin where Jason and Jeff were waiting for them.

The gear was quickly unloaded and carried inside the cabin - all except the cooler. It was left outside. The pot bellied wood stove had been fired up and any ice cubes left inside the cabin would melt. As Peabody and the Doc changed into their hunting clothes, Jason and Jeff began the friendly harassments that characterize hunting compadres.

"Where in hell have you been, Major? You're late. I expected you six minutes ago. Did you stop to enjoy the scenery? "

"I might just as well have. No reason to hurry. I'm told there are only seven Ruffed Grouse in Oconto County."

"You're wrong again. There are eight. I dunno if it's the cycle or the road hunters or if it's the turkeys. There are lots of turkeys around here. I think, maybe, they compete with the grouse for food and territory. I only know there aren't as many birds as there were last year"

"I see Doc Carmichael has been paroled. You don't care

who you associate with, do you, Major?"

Carmichael answered that one. "He brought me along to cure him from the dreadful diseases he's sure to contract from one or both of you."

* * * * *

The afternoon was unproductive. Jeff got a grouse. So did the Major. The next morning's hunt was worse. They saw a few birds, but didn't get much shooting. The noon meal was not punctuated by enthusiastic recollections of the morning activity. There was no bragging about long or tricky shots. No one was subjected to verbal keelhauling because of displays of miserable shooting. Few shots had been fired.

It was a group of subdued hunters who took to the field after lunch. Jeff and Jason followed what was once a logging trail. It ran more or less parallel to a small creek. Tag Alder grew on one side. On the other, there was enough sunlight to support grasses and occasional patches of clover.

The Major and Doc Carmichael elected to follow a narrow gauge railroad right-of-way that had been ripped up and abandoned after the cedar was logged off in the 1920s. It ran through a forty that had been clear cut four or five years ago. Young pople were growing there. They providing what would normally be excellent habitat for Ruffed Grouse.

Later in the afternoon, Carmichael grumbled his way back to the cabin. Jeff and Jason, equally unsuccessful, were already there.

"What did you get?" Jeff asked,

"What did I get? I'll tell you what I got. I got tired. I got back. I got bramble scratches. I got bitten by some kind of bug. I shot at a Woodcock and I don't want to talk about it."

"I heard five or six shots coming from your direction. Did

you and the Major have any luck?"

"I had luck," Doc Carmichael admitted. "It was all bad. I don't know about Peabody. We split up. He followed the South Branch and I looped around on the right-of-way. There must be a road up there somewhere. I think I heard a car. I suspect the shooting was from some damned road hunter. He probably got the only bird left in northern Wisconsin. No. There aren't any birds left in this county. He probably was shooting at tin cans."

"I think the Major got something," Jeff said. "I heard a couple of shots coming from his direction."

"Even if there were a few birds around, the trees are still full of leaves and Peabody would be lucky to get a shot off. I don't think there are any birds," Doc Carmichael repeated.

Jake disagreed. "I don't think that was a road hunter and I don't think it was target practice. The shots were too far apart. I'll bet Peabody got something," he said.

"I'll bet he comes back empty," Carmichael persisted. "The grouse are too spooky. They get nervous whenever it gets windy. They flush out of range. There are too many leaves to see them."

Jeff agreed with Jake. "The Major won't come back empty handed. I wouldn't be surprise if he got a limit."

Carmichael made no attempt to back away from his prediction and Jeff and Jake bullied him into making a wager. The terms of the bet were clear. If Peabody zeroed out, each of them would have to give the Doc fifty dollars, but for each grouse the Major brought back, Carmichael would have to give each of them fifty dollars.

To make sure he understood it, Jason said: "In other words, if Peabody comes in with only one bird, Jeff and I start making money and if he brings in five you owe each of us two hundred and fifty dollars. Right?"

"Well, yes, I guess," Carmichael slowly answered, clearly

showing he may have been a bit hasty when he made the bet.

Ten minutes later, Peabody appeared at the cabin door. When Doc Carmichael asked him if he had any luck, he replied in the affirmative. Jeff and Jason smiled. Carmichael frowned. Then Peabody emptied the contents of his hat on the table. "I found these honey mushrooms. They'll make a fine sauce. I hope you guys got some birds. I didn't see a thing." That was when Doc Carmichael smiled and Jeff and Jason frowned.

* * * * *

The next morning, Doc Carmichael and Major Peabody were in a jovial mood as they drove back to Green Bay. "We won a hundred bucks," Carmichael said. "Not bad. It'll pay for the gas and the car rental. What did you do with the grouse, Major?"

"I field dressed them and hid them under the ice in the cooler." Then the Major added: "Isn't it a beautiful day. Just look at that color. The woods are marvelous this time of year."

Impressions

Major Peabody waited until I had rung the bell to his apartment three times. I knew he was there. It was nearly eleven o'clock in the evening. I was preparing to perform my obligation to deliver his monthly Spendthrift Trust remittance. Peabody would be no place in the entire universe except in his apartment, waiting for me.

On the last day of the month, without fail, the Major invites me to dinner at some Philadelphia restaurant. The phrase "the Major invites me to dinner" is a euphemism meaning: Since I must deliver his check as soon as possible after midnight, I might as well spend the evening enjoying a leisurely meal with him at my expense. After dinner we usually retire to his apartment for conversation until the clock strikes twelve. After delivering his remittance, I am free to leave.

On the evening in question, that pattern had been broken. I was absent from Philadelphia while attending a two day seminar dedicated to tax reduction through intricate trust arrangements. I returned to town well after sundown. This meant I was unable to receive the Major's end-of-the-month telephone call inviting me to dinner. By keeping me waiting outside of his apartment door, Peabody was indicating his displeasure.

Finally, the door opened. Peabody's greeting was subdued. "Oh, it's you, counselor," he said. "You are tardy. I was concerned. I thought, perhaps, you had been arrested for committing some sadistic crime, disbarred and sentenced to a long term in prison, or, perhaps, one of you dissatisfied clients had, justifiably, murdered you."

I got the impression the Major was mildly displeased. Feeling somewhat guilty, I immediately explained my absence from the office and apologized for not advising him in a timely manner and for not rushing from the seminar before its conclusion in order to get back to Philadelphia in time to dine with him. The Major seemed mollified only after I made amends by inviting him to dinner on the following evening. Then, too late, it occurred to me that I had done nothing to require an apology.

Major Peabody has an almost uncanny ability to put me on the defensive. Whenever I point out one of his various derelictions of duty or violations of social grace, it always seems to end up with me apologizing to him. He's been getting away with it for years. I thought it was about time for me to strike back. Yes, it was time for me to turn the tables on him.

"Major," I said, "when you greeted me at the doorway, I received the distinct impression you thought I purposely avoided the dubious pleasure of taking you to dinner. Frankly, your conduct surprised me. Can it be that my impression was accurate?"

There, I thought. For a change I've put him on the defensive. I said no more. I waited for his explanation and for his apology. I was disappointed on both counts. I should have expected his response.

"And I, my young friend, am also surprised," he answered. "Surely you can't interpret my sincere concern for your safety and welfare to be an indication of displeasure. Surely my interest in your well-being should give you no cause to attack me."

He had done it again. I was back on the defensive. Before I could think of an appropriate cutting response, the Major

160

waved his hand as if to dismiss the mitigation I would certainly be expected to tender. He lit a cigar, sipped at a Scotch and water, leaned back in his chair and began a soliloquy.

"Don't apologize, young man," he said. "Impressions are often wrong. I remember a fellow who had been invited into our grouse camp a few years ago. He behaved well during the first day of our hunt and I was left with a favorable initial impression of him. I thought he deserved to be invited to join us in future hunts. Later in the evening, however, I was forced to change my opinion.

"After dinner, when the sun went down and the temperature dropped, the cabin began to cool and the wood box began to empty. That fellow actually moved his chair closer to the fire! Can you believe it?" Peabody slowly moved his head from side to side and said no more. I sat there, somewhat perplexed.

"And?" I questioned.

"And nothing," was the Major's answer. "The man should have gone outside to the wood pile and brought back an armful of wood to replenish the fire. By his inaction, he proved to me that he was, at best, of dubious character. My suspicions were later positively confirmed when I was told he was a Congressman.

"Impressions that have been built over a long period of time can be equally inaccurate. Jeffery Schultz is a case in point. Many believed Jeff was an insensitive, sarcastic, cynical, mean spirited son of a gun." (The Major did not say "gun".) "At least," the Major continued, "that was what his long time associates and closest friends called him. His enemies did not hold him in such high regard.

"I, on the other hand, had an entirely different impression of him. I had formed a favorable opinion of him and there was a good reason for my opinion. Jeff had a cabin and eighty wooded acres in northern Minnesota. When the Ruffed Grouse season opened, he always invited me to hunt with him. That, of course, is the mark of a true gentleman.

"On the morning of my first visit to Jeff's camp, I flushed a grouse twice - once on my way to the outhouse when I was unarmed and a few minutes later on my way back to the cabin. When I enthusiastically mentioned it to Jeff, he told me the hunting of that particular bird was strictly off limits.

"The grouse was Jeff's pet. It lived in a spruce thicket not more than thirty yards from the cabin door. Jeff asked me never to divulge the bird's existence, let alone its location. Of course, I honored his request. Many times, during our return to the cabin from subsequent hunts, we would flush that grouse, but even when game was scare, we never entered that thicket to look for it.

"Jeff and the grouse had an extraordinary relationship. He kept the bird supplied with corn and mushrooms, beetles, when he could find them, and an occasional apple. Jeff had become attached to the bird and the bird apparently liked him. It would often perch and spend the night on the balsam pole that served as a railing around the cabin's porch. For two years I watched that exceptional relationship of confidence and trust between man and bird.

"Last Spring I visited Minnesota and spent an evening reminiscing with Jeff. When I inquired of his pet grouse, he became somber. He explained what had happened. Toward the end of the previous year's bird season, Jeff was told the word of his pet grouse had somehow spread throughout the county. A group of hunters intended to invade Jeff's property when he was absent and shoot the bird.

"Jeff immediately tried everything he knew to chase his pet from the grove near his cabin. He yelled at it. He swore at it. He fired his shotgun in its general direction. Nothing worked.

The bond of friendship the grouse had established with Jeff could not be broken. The bird would not leave that small adjacent-to-the-cabin stand of spruce. Jeff faced the certain prospect of some grouse hunter killing his friend.

"My impression of Jeff's sensitive nature was then proven.

"Jeff frustrated the hunters' attempt to kill his pet. He, himself, shot and ate the bird."

Equality

I asked Major Nathaniel Peabody to accompany me to a Bucks County afternoon Garden Party. He begged off claiming he knew nothing about gardening and had no interest in learning about it. I told him the affair had nothing to do with gardening, that it was merely an outdoor social event.

I should have expected Peabody's reaction. He brought his eyebrows together, frowned ever so slightly, turned his head and stared at me for a few seconds. He didn't say a word. He didn't have to. His looks reminded me how uncomfortable he was in posh parties of the kind usually frequented by people who automatically disliked hunters. Unfortunately, I must admit, my circle of friends contains a goodly number of such folk.

I told him the lovely Stephanie wanted him to attend and in order to provide a special inducement, she had convinced the host to lay in a supply of ancient Macallan single malt Scotch. The Major had a soft spot in his heart for the lovely Stephanie. He seldom refused her invitations and reluctantly agreed to attend the event. He also liked 25 year old Macallan.

At the party I stayed close to the lovely Stephanie, but kept my eye on the Major as he circulated through the multitude. Though he solemnly promised to behave himself, I wanted to be able to get to him in a hurry if I saw any signs forecasting that he was about to commit some social outrage. I was surprised how well Peabody held up under the strain.

He complimented the host on the quality of the Macallan,

testing it from time to time. He was charming when introduced to ladies but, in each case, he quickly excused himself and carefully sought out the company of men with tanned, lined faces – the kind of men who looked like they might own shotguns and dogs.

He would often bump into a golfer or a tennis player by mistake. As in the case of the ladies, he would quickly move on, trying to find more satisfactory companionship. Peabody was in dangerous territory, but he successfully avoided skirmishes with anti-gun advocates and pseudo-environmentalists.

Later in the afternoon, the Major found two Scotch-drinking hunting-type compadres. With neckties removed or savagely loosened, they sat at a table shaded by a large multi-stripped umbrella. I noticed three women purposefully approach the Major and his friends. The trio was led by a tall, skinny woman, wearing sensible flat shoes and with carelessly attended, un-dyed hair, severely pulled into a bun at the back of her neck. I think she was trying to make some kind of statement. Later, I was told what then transpired.

As the women approach the table, the Major was rattling the ice cubes in his empty glass, hoping to attract the attention and remedial effort of one of his newly found friends. The leader of the ladies brigade came up from behind him and the tall, skinny one spoke.

"I suppose you will want one of us to refresh your drink and wait on you hand and foot," she said. There was no hint of humor or cordiality in her voice. Taken by surprise, the Major turned and made some innocuous comment. The lady disregarded it and began a confrontation by claiming she knew he had an unblemished history as an unreconstructed, male chauvinist.

"I don't believe we've met, madam" Peabody said, putting

the emphasis on the first syllable of the last word. "You falsely accuse me, MAdam," he said. "Of course, I believe in equal rights for women. To suggest otherwise distresses and is painful to me." The woman smiled, leaned toward him, stuck her chin out just a bit and informed him that she was a friend of his ex-wife and knew better. Peabody ignored the woman. He turned and addressed his new friends.

"The equality of the sexes is a concept I heartily endorse and recommend it be adopted by one and all. Had the idea of "Equal Rights" been universally adopted, the marriage to which the MAdam refers might have been saved. Unfortunately, it ended before the merits of the idea of equality between the sexes had been completely understood and accepted. Yes, I must admit, the MAdam is correct. My short term marriage ended in divorce.

"Like most men, I've never understood women. One of my friends gave a wedding present of three dozen Herter decoys. Looking back at it, I have the suspicion my ex did not appreciate the gift and, somehow, blamed me for her discontent. Strange." He paused and saw the men nod in agreement. He didn't see two of the women behind him throw unsmiling and thin lipped, but meaningful glances at Peabody's friends. He, however, did see the two women move to stand behind the men who, it turned out, were their husbands.

Ignoring the women, Peabody continued his discourse. "My wife brought the divorce action and it came as a surprise and disappointment to me." The Major then assigned the real cause of the divorce to his wife's failure to observe the concept of equality between the sexes.

"Given the fact that men and women are equal," he argued, "why should the bride receive wedding gifts which only she can use - gifts like silverware, kitchen utensils, scrub boards and the like? Peabody could feel the heat and animosity emanating from the tall, thin woman standing beside him. Nevertheless, he continued.

"Men and women are equal, period. Grooms should be able to get a wedding present of three dozen Herters decoys without repeated complaints from brides whose memories of such occurrences fade not but remain forever fresh and vibrant."

"My ex's Petition for Divorce claimed my association with smelly dogs, my terribly bloodthirsty shotgunning expeditions and what she described as my uncouth hunting associates had destroyed all potential for connubial bliss. Perhaps some of you may have witnessed the spouses of some of your friends voicing that same kind of trifling complaint?"

None of the men answered the question. They sat motionless, looking uncomfortable.

"Frankly, I thought she was being unfair," Peabody said. "I hadn't complained too bitterly when she hauled me off to cocktail parties where I was forced to associate with dilettante liberals. I hadn't objected too strenuously when she insisted I attend operas where tenors or sopranos would yell out many, many times that they were dying before that happy event occurred and the final curtain dropped. One properly aimed shot would have immediately finished off the singer and allowed the audience to return home 10 or 15 minutes earlier."

One of the men nodded vigorously until his wife elbowed him in the ribs.

"I put up with my wife's avocations," the Major said. "Being entirely committed to the philosophy of equality between the sexes, I expected she should put up with mine. I expected equal treatment from my wife but, obviously, she did not accept the philosophy of equality between the sexes."

Without turning to face her, Peabody told the tall skinny woman: "I hope, MAdam, this will set the record straight and destroy the canard that I am not in favor of equal treatment for women."

There was no response. The aggressive woman retreated and the other two wives hustled their husbands from the table, leaving the Major alone, gently rattling the ice cubes in his empty glass.

* * * * *

Two weeks later, Major Peabody got a telephone call from the men present during his confrontation with the tall, skinny woman at the Bucks County Garden Party. They extended a most cordial invitation to join them on a trip to Winisk on Hudson Bay. The goose hunting, they assured him, would be excellent.

Exercise

Some people have good health. They jog and watch their diet and take vitamins. Some of them work out on the beach or inside a gym. I don't go to the gym, but I believe it is important to exercise regularly. Each morning before breakfast, it is my usual practice to don a sweat suit and run the three mile course I've measured out from my apartment door.

The condition of Major Peabody's health concerns me. He shows no outward signs of deterioration, but I'm sure he would be healthier and happier if he would exercise. The Major, however, opposes such a suggestion. He considers exercise to be work and he doesn't enjoy work. When I explained my jogging regimen to him, he feigned astonishment. "How can you possibly enjoy good health if you have to work at it," he asked.

"It's good for me," I answered. "I'll live longer."

Peabody lit another Dominican Republic cigar, blew a line of smoke into the air and answered: "Oh? Are you sure? Your jogging exposes you to life threatening dangers. You might get hit by a speeding automobile as you run down the street. You might be mugged while running, alone and unarmed, in a city park. The police may see you running, presume you have committed some heinous felony and, as is their custom, shoot you dead without warning."

The best I could do in way of defense was to say: "Oh, come now, Major."

Peabody blew another cloud of smoke into the air. "If you

manage to evade those forms of early death," he said, "I suppose you might be able to add a few years to the time allotted to you by the mortality tables, but I wonder - is the game worth the candle? I doubt it." He took a pencil and a pad from the end table beside him and spoke to himself as he made some notations.

"Let's say it takes you an hour and a half to perform your despicable daily act of jogging. That would include preparation time, running time and the time you spend leaning against the side of your apartment building gasping for breath when you've finished your three mile course.

"One and a half hours a day - 365 days per year - 30 years," he murmured. He looked at the results of his calculation, nodded and said to himself: "I'll have to add a bit to take leap years into account and a bit more for the extra distances you'll have to run because of the times you are being chased by vicious dogs."

After a few more calculations, he handed me the pad and said, "There you have it young man. Study it. The conclusion is unmistakable. You'll spend about two years of your life jogging. That's about equal to the few years all that running will add to your life expectancy. It looks like a wash to me. Besides, you'll probably spend those extra two years strapped to a wheel chair in some nursing home, babbling and drooling on yourself."

What can you do with a man like that? He could buy a stationary bicycle or a home treadmill, but he won't. He spends all of his money on trips to Canada or Argentina or North Dakota or Maine, wasting good exercise time by walking miles over some tundra just to build a blind and shoot geese or by chasing a dog that's following a running pheasant when he could be staying in his apartment getting healthy exercise on a stationary bicycle.

As long as I'm complaining about him, I'll tell you something else. The Major doesn't visit a doctor for an annual check-up. I'm many years his junior and I go twice a year. He hunts with Doctor Carmichael. It wouldn't be a great inconvenience if he would drop in to the doctor's office from time to time. I've often tried to get him to make an appointment for a general physical. Those attempts have all been unsuccessful, but I persevere.

Last week, after a dinner at Bookbinders, we returned to his apartment for a night cap. I again took the opportunity to bring up the subject of exercise and its positive effects of Peabody's longevity. There was a reason for initiating that conversation. I had an ulterior motive. Come hell or high water, I intended to get the Major to schedule an appointment with Doctor Carmichael for a full physical examination.

"Young man," the Major said to me, "If you are to be insured of a long, happy and healthy life, there are three rules you must follow. First - You must assiduously avoid Funeral Directors. If you can push off all dealings with them for eighty or more years you will have attained the objective of longevity.

"The second rule is intended to insure your happiness. If you want to lead a life free from stress and trouble, you must avoid lawyers." Peabody noticed I winced and added: "Let me be clear. If you will recall the aphorism 'lie down with dogs, get up with fleas', you will never be tempted to associate with any lawyer who has abandoned private practice in favor of politics.

"Regarding attorneys engaged in private practice, there is good advice contained within the Italian proverb: 'A rat in the jaws of a cat is much better off than a client in the hands of a lawyer.' If you are to be happy, avoid all professional association with them, too. They are capable of committing terrible outrages - like withholding Trust Fund remittances."

I winced again and the Major noticed it again. "On a selective basis, however," he conceded in deference to me, "it's all right to dine and have social dealing with them. They tend to be pleasant companions in camp and in restaurants." I felt a bit better until he added: "They are especially welcome at the poker table where they have, very often, contributed to my happiness." I winced again.

"And, finally," he said, "my third rule is designed to promote good health and avoid premature aging. The rule is simple and easy to follow. To maintain a sound body, never seek out the services of the medical profession."

I now realized my task of getting Peabody to visit Doctor Carmichael would be doubly difficult. Nevertheless, I would not give up. Perhaps, I thought, I can appeal to his manhood. "Major," I said to him, "you can't really believe that. You aren't afraid to visit a doctor's office, are you? Is that it? Are you afraid of doctors?"

"Of course I'm afraid of doctors," he answered. "Any sane person is afraid of them. How many times have you seen someone visit a medico with some common complaint - like high blood pressure or chest pain. The doctor gives him some pills and scares the living bejaysus out if him. It doesn't take long before the poor fellow worries himself into a heart attack and dies.

"I've noticed," he went on, "that doctors never make mistakes when they diagnose an ailment. If they say you've got German measles, you die of German measles. Never mind the rumor that you also had malaria and tuberculosis." Peabody paused and studied the coal at the end of his cigar. "Do I need to point out," he observed, "that the attending physician is the one who fills out the death certificate."

It was obvious that all subtle suggestions to get the Major to agree to a medical examination were destined to fail. I decided to be blunt about the matter. "Major Peabody," I began, "When was the last time you visited a doctor? Isn't it about time you went to see Doctor Carmichael for a check-up?" I was surprised by his answer.

"For your information," he said. It was only three months ago." Then he blew a smoke ring. "Doc Carmichael said I had a particularly virulent, but then latent form of pneumonia. In his report he described me as a carrier - kind of a Typhoid Mary."

This was, indeed, disturbing news and I asked about his current state of health.

"Nothing to worry about," he answered. "I am in perfect health and I was in perfect health then, too. You see, it was the first week of the duck hunting season. After the judge read Carmichael's medical report, he excused me from jury duty and the Doc and I were able to go to Maryland for the opening day of the season."

I know when I'm beaten. I gave up.

Nightmare

"In answer to your question, my boy," said Major Nathaniel Peabody, "there are many reasons why a man hunts. In the millions of years following mankind's decision to supplement its diet of grass and roots with meat, hunting has been indelibly stamped into the psyche of everyone who is able to successfully capture birds and animals.

"Historically, Homo sapiens hunted only for food. With the advent of canned goods and super market grocery stores, the foodstuff motivation for the hunt has markedly declined. Nevertheless, man's primal urge to hunt has not been bred out of most of us. The people who have lost whatever it is that creates that urge will never be able to fully understand why men hunt.

"Moreover, there are still many good people who prefer meals of pheasant or wild duck or Ruffed Grouse or venison over meals of soy bean and chemical laced viands injected with artificial coloring to make them look palatable. I am one of them. You would be, too, if you carefully read the list of unnatural ingredients printed on the boxes of the junk sold in supermarkets.

"Of course, men hunt for many reasons other than securing healthful foods or following the ancient genetically stamped impulses that lead them to dogs and shotguns and fields and lakes and woods. Some men hunt to have an opportunity to 'knit up the raveled sleeve of care'. They want to get away from brain numbing television programs and talking head

174

newsmen who feel they must do their best to scare the hell out of them on a daily basis.

"The next earthquake will cause California to sink into the Pacific. Its screwball inhabitants will drown, polluting the sea and killing all the fish. A comet will strike the earth and we will all be in for it. The ice cap will melt, but New York City will not end up under water. The liberals will take over Congress. Everything you eat will cause cancer.

"If those threatened cataclysms aren't enough to cause an epidemic of diarrhea or bleeding ulcers, wives threaten you with additional dire consequences if you don't haul the garbage to the curb.

"Is it any wonder rational men want to get away from that kind of civilization induced stress and take a silent walk with a good dog in a field containing pheasants or seek out the peace of an early morning spent in a duck blind watching the sun rise or simply enjoy the beauty of the fall colors of a grouse covert, far from the madding crowd?"

The Major paused for a second before looking directly at me and adding: "There is also an advantage in getting away from people who persist in asking silly questions."

Being thus chastised for asking the question, I intended to let the matter drop, but Peabody wasn't inclined to do so. He blew a smoke ring and watched it float in the air. "In my own case," he continued, "I suspect a part of the reason for my attraction to shotgunning is my search for peace of mind. If I didn't have frequent opportunities to get away from people and cities, I'm afraid I might become vituperative, sarcastic, anti-social, and develop curmudgeon-like tendencies."

I did not make any of the more obvious comments.

"We live in an era when too many people insist on controlling our lives," he said. "So-called experts, social engineers, weird college professors and high school drop-out actors insist they know what is best for all of us. If our wimpy politicians think they can gain a single vote by doing it, they will support and pass the most insane legislation. Unless we have occasional opportunities to call "Time Out" and develop a healthy sense of skepticism, we run the risk of becoming brainless sponges, absorbing as truthful whatever nonsense is thrown at us."

"And," I ventured, "just what has all of that that got to do with why you hunt?"

"The point is so obvious," Peabody responded, "it doesn't need explanation. Let me explain it to you. When I am hunting no one can tell me I can't enjoy a cigar or own a 20 ga. Lefever or relax with a glass of The Macallan. I even have the ability to descry the movement toward monolithic government without fear of being pilloried or accused of holding politically improper attitudes and sentenced to a term in prison. Hunting puts me in an environment where I can experience a feeling of freedom and, my young friend," he continued, "this country wasn't made by social engineers and bureaucrats. The men who tamed the wilderness did it without much help from them."

"Like Lewis and Clark's Voyage of Discovery?" I said.

"Exactly like Lewis and Clark's Voyage of Discovery," the Major answered. "That was a time in our history when men were on their own. Lewis and Clark's expedition wasn't subjected to governmental micromanagement. They organized their expedition without some bureaucrat telling them what to do. Imagine the fun they must have had. Unfettered exploration. I wish I had been with them."

That night Major Nathaniel Peabody had a nightmare.

* * * * *

"How are you Nate?" the President asked as he arose from his desk and extended his hand in greeting.

"I'm fine, Red," Major Peabody responded. Only President Thomas Jefferson's closest friends called him 'Red'. "Well, perhaps I'm not so fine," the Major admitted. "I'm having trouble with this Voyage of Discovery thing."

Jefferson was having his own troubles. Some people thought he paid too much for the Louisiana Purchase. The press was attacking him. Protesters were marching in the streets. They were carrying signs like: 'Jefferson Just Wants a City In Missouri Named After Him.'

"What is it, Major?" the President asked. "Do you need more money? I don't think we can expect much from Congress. Damned politicians! Most of them are only interested in re-election. A bunch of Senators are already raising Cain. Half of them want to get rid of me. Some say I wasn't properly authorized to buy anything from Napoleon. They want to have hearings and start an investigation."

"It's not a matter of money, Red," the Major said. "There's so much pork in the budget Congress has authorized that I could fund a rocket expedition to the moon. The Voyage of Discovery should come in well under Congressional estimates. I've got plenty of money, but I've run into a lot of other problems.

"First of all, the OSHA people won't give their approval to the project. They want me to carry eighty more oars in case the boys break or lose some. They want me to provide every man with a Coast Guard approved life jacket. They insist every man be issued a supply of sun block and Polaroid glasses to protect them from ultra violet rays. Ultra violet rays! Hell, Red, they haven't even been discovered yet.

"That's just the tip of the iceberg. If I tried to carry half the stuff OSHA is requiring, I'd have to rebuild the boat. It would be so big the boys wouldn't be able to pole it up the river. Talk about a Catch 22. They won't let us leave St. Louis unless we have a boat so big that we can't leave St. Louis.

"That's not all. The EPA is giving me fits.

"They want an Environmental Impact Study and won't let me go until they get one. Environmental Impact Study! Impact on what? Nobody knows what's out there. How on earth can we give them an impact study when no one knows what is going to be impacted? Another Catch 22, Red. The EPA wants an Impact Study before they'll let me leave St Louis and I can't give them an Impact Study unless I leave St. Louis and get to the places where the 'impact' is to be 'studied.'"

President Jefferson looked out the window and mused, "I like that phrase, 'Catch 22', Nate. I sure hope it will some day inspire Joseph Heller to write a novel and use it as the title." Major Peabody disregarded him and continued with his litany of complaint.

"The only success I can report," he said, "is with the EEOC. I've made a deal with Toussaint Charbonneau. He's a French trapper. He'll come with me and bring one of his wives along. She's a Shoshone Indian woman named Sacagawea. That will take care of both of the EEOC's ethnic and gender diversity objections.

"I suspect I'll have some kind of a Union problem. The Barge Polers, Beaver Skinners and Mountain Men's Local #1739 is trying to organize us. If they're successful, I'm sure they want to cut us down to 12 hour days and you know what that will do to out time schedule. And how in hell am I going to provide health and dental care when I'm half way up the Columbia River?

"To make matters worse, today I got a certified letter from the anti-gun people. I'm sure you know all about them. They're the ones who argue that if the Minute Men didn't have guns, they wouldn't have killed all those Brits at Concord, Lexington and Breed's Hill. Their letter says they're going to raise absolute hell if we take muskets, side arms, knives or swords with us. They claim they have a lot of support from Massachusetts politicians. Massachusetts, of all places! Have they forgotten so soon?

"I'd hate to see the Brits or the Russians or the Spaniards take control of the West Coast, Red, but I've had it right up to here with the politicians, the special interest groups and the bureaucrats. The only reason I agreed to head up this expedition was because of the reports of the great dove and Prairie Chicken hunting out on the plains. If I can't bring a shotgun with me, I'm not going. I hate to leave you in the lurch, Red, but I QUIT."

Then the Major put on his coonskin hat and left the White House.

It's Not All Roses

As an attorney in the Trust Department of Smythe, Hauser, Engals and Tauchen, one of Philadelphia's prestige law firms, I prepare complex documents intended, for the most part, to govern post-mortem distributions of large amounts of money. I therefore deal with people who own large amounts of money.

One such client was William Henry Peabody. Sensitive to his son's profligate ways, he created the Peabody Spendthrift Trust. William Henry has gone to his reward. The beneficiary of the Trust, Major Nathaniel Peabody, is the black sheep of that prominent and affluent family. Though he is not affluent, (certainly not affluent at the end of the month) Nathaniel Peabody somehow seems much happier than my moneyed clients.

To tell the complete truth (something an attorney will occasionally do) I think I envy him. He owns no real estate or automobile so he doesn't automatically think all plumbers and auto mechanics are members of Ali Baba's team of forty thieves. He has no dog or wife to feed or maintain or take to the veterinary clinic. His tax returns are uncomplicated. He has no reason to follow the stock market or worry about its fluctuations.

Major Peabody has no need to plan the management of his income for periods longer than 31 days. Though often penniless as the end of a month approaches, he knows his Spendthrift Trust remittance will, like the cavalry, arrive in the nick of time to save him on the first day of the ensuing month.

Last week at the office, I momentarily stopped trying to analyze one of the various incomprehensible provisions of the U S Tax Code and looked out the window at the blowing February snow storm. I was working under stress. I was living in a cold, gray unattractive clime. Peabody was in Mexico, probably enjoying a Margarita while stretched out in the sun next to some 5 Star hotel pool, filled with Latin beauties. He was, I concluded, the luckiest man in the world.

Then Charlotte brought the mail and I found an envelope with a Mexican postage stamp. I opened it, read it and realized the Major, too, had his problems.

* * * * *

Dear Counselor:

This expedition has been a complete disaster. It began on a very bad note. Jerry and Alice Koenig invited me to spend the evening in their home. The plane left very early in the morning and Jerry had agreed to take me to the airport.

Of course, I brought a small token of my appreciation to recognize their kindness. That small token took the form of a bottle of single malt Scotch whisky. While browsing in a liquor store, I came upon a brand name previously unknown to me. It is called "Sheep Dip" and is an eight year old unblended product. In a moment of whimsy, I bought it and delivered it to my hostess.

Now, please understand, neither of the Koenigs drank Scotch. From time to time, I brought them quality distillations of that product, secure in the knowledge that they would never drink any of it and I would have a secure supply of acceptable libation whenever I visited them. However, buying the Sheep Dip was grievous error.

Alice and Jerry were quite taken by the name and label, so they decided to sample it. They liked it. Now they drink Scotch, including the stuff I leave with them as tokens of my appreciation. I have unwittingly destroyed a watering hole where I was previously assured of an appropriate supply of appropriate drinking material.

With that kind of a beginning, I should have suspected a disaster of even greater magnitude awaited me. At the airport, I dropped my suitcase on my great toe and, during the flight, the pain increased. I was limping when I met Jim Zimmerman in the Dallas airport. He was to be my hunting companion.

We changed planes and, together, flew to Santa Cruz. When we arrived at Santa Cruz, my toe was swollen and it hurt. I no longer limped. I hobbled. I had to carry my own baggage through Customs, to the taxi, into the Colonial Hotel and up the stairway to our room. Every step was an agony.

This morning, with difficulty, I could get out of bed, but I couldn't get a stocking on my foot - let alone a walking boot. That offending toe, I am convinced, knows the location of every nerve in my right leg. Whenever I move my foot, I pay for it. I missed breakfast and explained my condition to Zimmerman. After assuring me that my agony might possibly cause him a sleepless night, he happily left for the shooting fields.

Zimmerman is excessively enjoying my discomfort. He finds it delightful - so delightful that I have reassessed my opinion of him. I am now convinced that he has only one redeeming quality. He holds the mistaken opinion that he is capable of successfully playing Cribbage for money.

The Colonial Hotel is a Half Star Hotel located on the outskirts of Santa Cruz. As the name implies, it must have been built during the colonial period - the early colonial period. It has two storeys, twenty rooms and a questionable water supply.

It is more than adequate if you are interested in a quick meal and a place to sleep between hunts. It is not the place to spend time if the slightest touch or movement of the big toe is a cause of great pain.

When not rented to the unwary, I'm sure the management uses this room as a breeding ground for rats which, I suspect, are sold to laboratories for experimentation purposes. By the looks of this place, they must enjoy voluminous sales and are probably making a mint off the project.

In response to my numerous requests, a hotel doctor appeared late in the afternoon. We had an interesting conversation.

"I believe I have broken my toe. This one." (I pointed at it.)

This one?" he asked and touched it.

"OUCH. Yes."

"Hmmmmmmmmmmmm"

"Should I put ice on it?"

"Yes. That might be good."

(End of consultation.)

In a little while the maid brought me two kinds of pills, a supply of ice and an ice pack. In response to my request, she brought me reading material (a biography of Francisco "Pancho" Villa, written in Spanish) and a tall glass. From time to time, I very carefully take ice from the ice pack, put it into the tall glass and add some single malt Scotch to kill any microbes that might be in the ice. From time to time, she returns to bring more ice.

When Zimmerman came back from the afternoon hunt, he spent too much time telling me the shoot was magnificent and explaining its joy in detail. He showered and left after announcing he was going to a restaurant famed for its cabrito asado. He said he'd stop at the local MacDonalds and bring me a hamburger in case I wanted a midnight snack.

I am alone, listening to the pitty-pat of falling water. It is not raining. Water is dripping from the shower head in the bathroom and I can't get up to tighten the damned faucet.

I'm laying on my back with my bare foot resting on a towel. It is bare because my big toe violently objects to the weight of a sheet that might otherwise cover it.

I'm trying to keep that toe entirely motionless. The task is complicated by the swarm of resident flies that insist upon constantly crawling all over it.

Lord knows what tomorrow will bring.

Peabody

Other Books by Galen Winter

500 WILD GAME AND FISH RECIPES (Editor)

LEGENDARY NORTHWOODS ANIMALS -
A Farcical Field Guide

BACKLASH - A Compendium of Lore and Lies (Mostly Lies)
Concerning Hunting, Fishing & the Out-Of-Doors

THE BEST OF THE MAJOR

THE AEGIS CONSPIRACY

BACKLASH II - Tales Told by Hunters, Fishermen
and Other Damned Liars

CPSIA information can be obtained
at www.ICGtesting.com
Printed in the USA
BVHW071454281021
620031BV00001B/7